Keep Walking...

Hebrews 3:14
...Walking Steadfast to the End

Short Messages for Bold Faith

Mary Pat Jones

Keep Walking...

Mary Pat Jones

April 2017

Published: Linda Lange Resources
Life Application Ministries
P.O. Box 165
Mt. Aukum, CA 95656
www.lindalange-resources.com

Cover Picture: Janet Odella
Cover Design: Linda Lange

Printer: createspace.com

Permission is granted to use this material for teaching and ministry purposes providing proper credit is given to its source and it is not sold for profit.

A Grateful Heart

Of course it's common to write an "acknowledgment" page, but somehow that word didn't seem to fit for me. I want to say so much more than just "acknowledge" those who have walked by my side in this journey.

First and foremost, I would like to humbly thank my husband Rick. God raised him up and put him in my life when I needed him most. In all the loss, Rick held God's hand and held mine and wasn't going to let go of either of us. As I poured out my thoughts in these written messages, he would read, edit and encourage me to keep going. He was my Aaron, holding my arms up when I could have slipped into never-never land. We cried when we should have been laughing, and laughed when it would have made more sense to cry. We got through and came out on the other side, just like the Hebrew boys coming out of the fire, untouched, and just like Jesus, simply getting up out of the tomb. We walked through death and came out on the other side. I call it horrifically wonderful. Horrific because it was; wonderful, because God is bigger than death and showed us that often!

I want to thank Linda Lange with Life Application Ministries who started this process in the first place when Rick won a grand prize at her conference of publishing a book. It was never something I wanted to do, but God had other plans. Her encouragement, expertise and heart for helping others through the writing and publishing process was gratefully accepted and appreciated. I highly recommend that you check out her ministry!!

To Gretchen—my best friend—the one who journeyed with me in the salvation process. We got to meet God and know God in a deep and intimate way when God put a hunger in us that only the Bread of Life could satisfy. I could not and would not have done this book had she not agreed to read and edit all, and I mean all of the written newsletters that I had accumulated. I wrote those newsletters from my heart and my heart didn't want to edit! She painstakingly went through each one and made them readable to all. I pray God would bless her in His greatest way and that as friends that we would grow to be more like Him.

I want to also thank Martha and Suzy for their invaluable support in making this happen. You are true friends.

And to all my dogs – thanks for taking me on so many walks whereby I could pray and think and worship God.

Truly I say to you all...keep walking!

INTRODUCTION

Short Messages for Bold Faith

Psalm 61:2 *...when my heart is overwhelmed: lead me to the rock that is higher than I.*

Thank you for joining me in this journey that I didn't want to take. If that sounds like you, then perhaps there is a "God" reason as to why you are reading this. I had become a "real" Christian in 1999 after being raised in a nice religious background—also known as a dead church. God then graciously delivered me from depression and addictions, then took me on a wonderful journey of truly knowing Him. It was good!

In 2008, He decided to do further work in my life. I had actually been praying for God to "mature me as a believer." He answered that prayer and continues to do so in what eventually became known as "Creative Footage—a story unfolding" ministry.

On September 21, 2008, I received a shocking call that my oldest son, Forrest, had committed suicide. He had gotten through all the rough patches of growing up with a single mom. He even made it through the Army and was working as a professional custom carpenter which was his dream job. Somehow, life on this earth wasn't enough and his life on this earth was over. A week later, to the day and hour, we received another horendous call saying Dustin, my youngest son had been in a tragic accident and lay in a neurotrauma unit, paralyzed from the neck down and on a ventilator. Five weeks later, my mother who was a rock in my life, died unexpectedly from cancer.

With so many sudden trials, I was determined to stand for God and not go down into the pit. I knew I was

Keep Walking...

in a battle. It would have been easy to fall back into old behaviors and thought patterns, but shuffling around in pink fuzzy slippers in a psych ward was not my idea of God getting any glory out of my life. I was like a two-year-old with hands on her hips saying "no" to a devil that wanted to snuff me out. All I knew was "no," but I wasn't really sure of the "how." I started wondering how I could best serve the Lord through this situation.

What you are about to read is the "how." Since scripture tells us to become more like Jesus, I knew that I would need to know Him in a deeper, more profound, and intimate way. I knew He had the answers I needed to help me walk right through death and emerge without a hint of smoke on me. I had to really "know" how Jesus could walk through every trauma, sin and devastation with me and still have joy along the way. I didn't want to lose my long sought after joy in the midst of all the loss. Depression and addictions were not the answer. They didn't work before and they sure wouldn't going to work here.

I began to study this Jesus through the word and to observe how He handled life. The result of my desperate quest for more of Him, His wisdom and joy, were these messages written as weekly newsletters. The messages were for me but I eagerly shared them with others, in person and online. I wrote for three years through the holidays, through the seasons and often from words of a song. You may be reading a July 4th message in February or a Christmas message in May. Just relax and prayerfully enjoy them as daily application to your life. Seasons come and go, but we can always change with the Lord. You may need to celebrate freedom in October, or a resurrection in a wintery area of your life. You may want to sit back and listen to the song from which a message to me was incubated.

Unfortunately, my youngest son died less than a year later of complications from the accident. During that

Keep Walking..

year, I had learned to celebrate the Victory over death that Jesus experienced on my behalf. My time praying and studying His word bore fruit, I "knew" Him. I offered up many prayers during this time and God always answered with two simple words "keep walking."

Please know that in the midst of death (be it death of a bad habit, a career or relationship loss etc) there is life. If you say "yes" to the invitation of Jesus, you will receive Him in His fullness. This life in Him can't be managed or controlled, but only received. He will grow in you, and stretch you, and change you and perhaps frighten you a bit out of complacency. But in the end, life will flow consistently from you. For those who have welcomed Jesus can welcome death, because in death there are no periods, only commas.

Keep walking...

Rejoicing in the Fire

Dearly "Beloved" (that's you in case you don't know!), what a pleasure to study the very verse that God shared with me when I began to question Him about "what the deal was" and what eventually became the title of my book "Walking through Fiery Trials."

So here we go, plant this in your brain where it can always be there whenever you might need to be reminded about "why" you are going through what you are going through.

1 Peter 4:12-13 *Beloved, think it not strange concerning the fiery trial which is to try you, as though some strange thing happened unto you: But rejoice, inasmuch as ye are partakers of Christ's sufferings that, when His glory shall be revealed, ye may be glad also with exceeding joy.*

When I was writing the "No Shuffling" workbook, I realized the irony of the Word. I mean really, "rejoice" when you are going through fiery trials? That seems wrong by the world's standard, but in God's way He seems to be trying to say, "Just hang in there girl, fiery trials will always be there and so will I, so just rejoice and watch me carry out the greatest plan ever made."

When we can realize how much He took on so that we would not be condemned to live in hell forever, then our bit of hell on earth really does humble us as we "partake" of some of what He had to walk through. But the advantage we have is that He shows us how to come out on the other side. His example of walking towards the most horrific death, visiting hell so we don't have to for eternity, and then coming out to live forever is what we need to focus on. That is a promise to the believer as well. We never have to fear that things won't change, because all of His promises are "yes and amen." Will they

Keep Walking..

all be this week, or next year or even while we are here on earth?

I think the answer is some yes and some we may have to wait for when we go to live with Him. But know you never have to fear, that you won't get healed, or that your broken heart won't rejoice anymore, or that relationship won't be mended. He's simply enough.

I heard this piece of good advice, "Don't ask God the "why and the reasons," instead rely on the "who and the relationship." It will serve you far better!!

Thank you for participating with me in walking through this thing called life. I love having your arms on both sides of me while our Shepherd leads us.

Let us be good sheep and follow!!

Keep Walking...

DO VS. DONE

I want to talk about legalism as I have been studying the book of Galatians. Legalism teaches that justification (my favorite definition —"just like your sin didn't happen") and sanctification depends upon our own works. Boy I am tired already! I believe legalism is the greatest hindrance to us receiving our freedom in Christ. After all, most of the Pharisees didn't get it.

Religious law says "do," Jesus says "done."

So what are examples of us as Christians trying to keep the modern day law so frequently found in the church? I guess we could sum it up in the statement, "I have to do this, I should do that, I need to be doing more." That really was the whole purpose of the law, to show us we couldn't do it all and we needed a Savior who fulfilled the law. If we can earn salvation and be sanctified by obedience to the law, then the Cross is redundant.

Galatians 2:21 *I do not frustrate the grace of God; for if righteousness come by the law, then Christ is dead in vain.*

We are afraid to be free of the law. We don't trust ourselves to make choices led by the Spirit of God, so we revert back to the false comfort of the law. That is exactly what happened in Galatians 3:1 when Paul asks them, "Who hath bewitched you?" One set of notes I read said, "The Judaizers are like evil sorcerers diverting their victims eyes from the Cross to the Law." In the study of the Greek word "bewitched," it means to fascinate with false representation. That has always been a profoundly powerful statement to me to describe the law. The bewitching power behind the law comes to tell you to follow it and only draws you to a never ending life of work, condemnation and lack of joy.

Keep Walking..

The law is always telling you that you and what you do for God, and others is never enough. It is a "snake charmer" so graceful and looking good only to bite and poison you and wait for the next victim.

Don't frustrate the grace of God and make Christ's death all vanity. Give up the oppression and fear of "trying" to be good and receive Him. You are not good, and God knows that. He doesn't expect a perfect person, otherwise he could have made us all robots. What He does want is your heart. No, I take that back, He wants all of you: the good, the bad, the impatient, the talents, the lack, the everything. Only then can He mold you into His image. God doesn't waste anything. Give Him your all so He can use it for His glory. Read Jeremiah 18 about the potter. When the pot was cracked he didn't throw it away, he just put it back on the wheel. Your past, present and future may have to visit the wheel, but don't fret, it is God's hands that cover it all.

Ask God to reveal some of your personal religious laws that have robbed the basic message of the gospel from you. It so grieves our Father who sacrificed His Son so we could be free from the law.

Be free in Him.

Keep Walking...

ONLY RECEIVE

I want to take just a minute and comment upon something that recently escaped from my mouth! I said, "When you realize, and I mean really realize, what God did in sending Jesus to take away all of our sin, it is so humbling and in a sense almost suffocating." I thought back about that and asked myself if "suffocating" was really the right word.

The Bible talks about the "glory of God" over and over. I think I could study this forever. I found that in the old testament the glory could depart (1 Samuel 4:21), that God is our glory (Psalm 62:7) and the glory of God conceals things (Proverbs 25:2). I also found that we were created for His glory:

Isaiah 43:7 *Even every one that is called by my name: for I have created him for my glory, I have formed him; yea, I have made him.*

The word "glory" in the Hebrew means "weight/heavy pressure but in a good sense." So the glory of God can be understood as suffocating, like a heavy weight bearing down on us—but it is positive. Get a visual for that and you will find that what God has done for us is very humbling.

If I came and cooked you dinner and cleaned your house, you probably would want to repay me. For most of us, we would want to give something in return so you thought we were on top of our game plan, or you wouldn't think we were needy, or not grateful or any number of other thoughts.

It is very hard to receive something of value and not do anything but receive, but yet that is what Christ did for us. He expects nothing in return except relationship. No spiritually or otherwise driven works; just us. That

Keep Walking..

is hard and that is why it seems almost overwhelmingly suffocating to receive that.

Now, when you feel like you are suffocating, what do you do? You gasp for breath. Don't you know that is exactly what He wants us to do? Breathe in Him, the "pneumo" or breath of the Spirit of God. We can then see how this glory thing is a positive weight if we will just breathe. And yes it is overwhelming.

Big hugs, walking and breathing...

Keep Walking...

Joining in the Song

We all have songs that will often show up in our minds and we find ourselves singing their tune. I would like to share one that has become a prayer of mine when I just can't seem to find the words to pray.

It is taken from the following scripture:

Zephaniah 3:17 *The LORD thy God in the midst of thee is mightly; he will save, he will rejoice over thee with joy; he will rest in his love, he will joy over thee with singing.*

I have been using the word "appropriate" in my own walk with what God has done through Jesus. It is very important to have a complete understanding of this word. It means to take possession of. It is with this scripture that I want you to "appropriate" the fact that God is singing over you. Now if that is not a comforting lullaby, I am not sure what is.

The song I would like to share was written out of a heart (Christy Nockels) that heard about human trafficking and brothels and how the women would take their babies and put them under the bed while they made their money. We don't have any idea how people who have suffered extreme trauma come out of it with any of their senses intact. These "things," if you are exposed to will actually change you forever for good, if you allow it. It motivates us to reach out like only Jesus could do, removes any of our own self pity and will give us a heart of gratitude and prayer. It is then that we can sing these words and know that only God can be mighty in their/our midst, that He will save us, rejoice over us and allow us to rest in Him. Now that is a song!!

The words are powerful when you line them up with the Zephaniah scripture. It is a cry when everything seems so devastating to have God wrap His arms around

Keep Walking..

us, to hear our faintest cry, for Him to continue singing these songs of deliverance and love over us and most importantly for us to join Him and sing along. Here I go again with that "intercourse" word I seem to use so much lately. Can we literally "join" Him, believing in the power of His songs over us and receive all that He is, can, and will do for us that believe? It is His heart for us to appropriate, have intercourse or become one with Him in all things for His and our good. His Word is the only thing that can prosper and make a difference in these hideous situations. There is hope - please sing along for yourself and others.

Psalm 32:7 *"Thou art my hiding place; thou shalt preserve me from trouble; thou shalt compass me about with songs of deliverance. Selah."*

Christy Nockels - Sing Along [Passion 2012] Lyrics

From babies hidden in the shadows

To the cities shining bright

There are captives weeping

Far from sight

For every doorway has a story

And some are holding back the cries

But there is one who hears at the night

Great God

Wrap your arms around this world tonight

Around the world tonight

And when you hear our cries

Sing through the night

So we can join in your song

And sing along yeah,

We'll sing along...

Keep listening...

Keep Walking...

SIMPLY GRACE

I am stuck on a comment I heard that said, "Grace is key to our victory, not our own ability to fight spiritual battles." My background is always been to "do" something. In the past I relied on my own strength through college degrees, exercise, perfect nutrition or whatever might be the latest false hope. In the more recent past, I have focused on having the proper "knowledge" to fight the devil.

For God's grace (which is defined in the Greek as "His divine influence on our hearts and the reflection in our life) to win the battle, and for us to do nothing but believe and accept, is often hard for us to wrap our worldly, legalistic minds around. We all have a hard time giving ourselves up!

James 4:6-7 *But he giveth more grace. Wherefore he saith, God resisteth the proud, but giveth grace unto the humble. Submit yourselves therefore to God. Resist the devil, and he will flee from you.*

When we focus on what we have done right or wrong, we are performance centered and we don't believe what Jesus did for us. Simply put... we don't receive Him or the purpose of the Cross.

We may throw up a prayer for God to get us through our problem, but then in our own pride we get busy looking for a solution! We repent, we rebuke, we fast, we pray, we read spiritual books. If the enemy can get us performance focused, then we would go under condemnation and the devil wins. God "resisteth" those who try to win spiritual battles, what He calls "the proud." Instead it is His grace that we submit to, His grace that helps us resist the devil and His grace for us of what He did on the cross that causes the enemy to flee. Satan is defeated don't forget!!

Keep Walking..

1 Peter 5:5-6 *"Likewise, ye younger, submit yourselves unto the elder. Yea, all of you be subject one to another, and be clothed with humility: for God resisteth the proud, and giveth grace to the humble. Humble yourselves therefore under the mighty hand of God, that he may exalt you in due time:"*

I think we need to change our prayers saying: Lord, instead of removing the problem like I want, and me doing what I think You want me to do, I am going to humble myself and submit to your grace. When I think that it is me that is qualified to win in spiritual warfare, it can become pride. In reality I have nothing to win this battle but You and in reality that is all I ever needed or wanted. The devil lied to me and said it was up to me to keep all the law. It is only through my inability to keep the law that he can come and condemn me and get me into all types of works. God, I want to resign from myself and depend on your grace. You came to fulfill the law because you knew I would never be able to. I want to allow myself to really trust your grace and mercy. Let me rest in you and allow you to influence my heart in the direction of your perfect answer. Thank you that You do not say that it is my works, spiritual or otherwise, that will help me in my time of need but your grace—I am humbled.

Hebrews 4:16 *Let us therefore come boldly unto the throne of grace, that we may obtain mercy, and find grace to help in time of need.*

I am so trying to understand that when I need something, I need to ask for His grace and nothing else. Again, His "divine influence on my heart and the reflection of Him in me" is the working of the cross and the Holy Spirit that He so generously left me when He went home to be with the Father...

So simple, so profound!

GET UP!

What a blessing all of the resurrection messages have had on my heart the past few weeks. He is risen! The cross couldn't hold him, the grave couldn't keep Him and death wasn't enough—He got up!!!! That is a verse from a favorite song of mine and always encouraged me when I was going through a funk. I would say out loud, "If Jesus can get up from what He just endured, I certainly can too!" NO whining!!

If we really take a minute to reflect we realize that most of our troubles are self-induced. We meditate on our woes and because we have such an excellent neurological system, those little "woe" neurons grow and make a little pathway that keep reminding us how tough our life is. What is the answer? Of course, it is to meditate on God's Word and get those little neurons all fired up. They get stronger and stronger and the little "woe" neurons start losing strength because they are not being used.

There you have it, a brief synopsis of the neurology behind walking out of our old patterns. Your neurons need three things to grow - oxygen, nutrients and stimulation. Your thoughts are the stimulation. Get your mind on the Word of God and watch your life change. God knew all of this neurology stuff when Joshua 1:8-9 was written.

Joshua 1:8-9 *This book of the law shall not depart out of thy mouth; but thou shall meditate on it day and night, that thou mayest observe to do according to all that is written therein: for then thy shall make thy way prosperous, and then thou shalt have good success. Have not I commanded thee? Be strong and of good courage, be not afraid, neither be thou dismayed: for the Lord thy God is with thee withersoever thou goest.*

Keep going...

Keep Walking..

No Fretting!

I used to attend a wonderful church in Naples, Florida and I will always remember a guest speaker that preached a sermon called "Fret Not, Fret Not, Fret Not" which was taken from **Psalm 37**:

Verse 1 - *Fret not thyself because of evil doers, nether be thou envious against the workers of iniquity.*

Verse 7 - *Rest in the Lord and wait patiently for him: fret not thyself because of him who prospereth in his way, because of the man who bringeth wicked devices to pass.*

Verse 8 - *Cease from anger, and forsake wrath: fret not thyself in any wise to do evil.*

If you look up the word "fret" in the Hebrew language it means to be hot; furious; to burn; to be angry. Now if God says it three times, I think it commands our attention.

God tells us that rather than getting all angry and fired up we should rest in Him and wait patiently. That is nice until our world falls apart and we are forced to live in confusion and agony like so many other people. Is it possible to rest in Him? Fretting causes harm, it can cause us to do evil.

I am prompted by Oswald Chamber's July 4th devotional in his book "My Utmost for His Highest." He says, "It is one thing to say, "Do not fret," but something very different to have such a nature that you find yourself unable to fret."

Oswald Chambers goes onto say, "If the "Do not" doesn't work there (in confusion and agony), then it will not work anywhere." Our "Do not" (fret) must work during our days of difficulty and uncertainty as well as our good days, or it will never work."

Keep Walking...

And lastly, hold on, as this is a real zinger. He makes the statement, "We tend to think that a little anxiety and worry are simply an indication of how wise we really are, yet it is actually a much better indication of just how wicked we are. Fretting rises from our determination to have our own way." I guess each day I am coming more and more into an understanding that I don't have to figure out God's way, but just to trust Him in His infinite wisdom.

"Lord, help me to keep looking up. It is when I look to the left and right that I begin that slippery road down to fear, worry, anger and all the other things that are designed to steal my peace, my health and my relationships. You make it so simple. I just need to look up. Help me to focus on the only thing that can bring me through anything with my senses intact and give me wisdom and peace within all situations; and that is a deep and passionate and intimate relationship with Jesus."

Look up, keep walking.

No Smell of Smoke!

Good morning, good afternoon, good evening to you all.

It is all good unless we make the enemy of our mind lord of our thoughts. God said it was "very good" so who are we to listen to something that says otherwise?

I was reading in Oswald Chambers' book, "My Utmost for His Highest," and I love it when you read something that you have experienced or thought and someone else has put it into eloquent words. He was writing about 2Cor 4:8-10.

2 Corinthians 4:8-10 *We are troubled on every side, yet not distressed; we are perplexed, but not in despair; Persecuted, but not forsaken; cast down, but not destroyed; Always bearing about in the body the dying of the Lord Jesus, that the life also of Jesus might be made manifest in our body.*

Oswald Chambers says, "The only thing that will enable me to enjoy adversity is the acute sense of eagerness of allowing the life of the Son of God to evidence itself in me. Our circumstances are the means God uses to exhibit just how wonderfully perfect and extraordinarily pure His Son is. Discovering a new way of manifesting the Son of God should make our heart beat with renewed excitement."

We need to keep our soul (mind, will, emotions, and thoughts) properly conditioned to walk through fiery trials with our hand in God's hand. Really the only other choice is ranting and raving or delving into self pity or choosing something to numb us.

Remember the Hebrew boys in the fire? The greatest statement I think they made was in Daniel 3:17-18 saying they were confident in the God that they served believing that He would deliver them from the fiery furnace... but then verse 18 says, *"But if not, be it known unto thee, that we will not serve thy gods..."* They weren't afraid of the fire! God would either deliver them or not. They were concerned about standing for God and not bowing down to a sinful life of oppression and hopelessness if they worshiped the golden image.

I remember my first thought when the trials of losing my sons came, and that was, "Lord, how do I represent You in this situation?" You know I am not some spiritual giant, I just remembered the story of Shadrach, Meshach and Abednego. I too wanted to come through the fire without the smell of smoke. When people get around you and begin to know your situation, are they hacking from all the smoke, or is the "life of Jesus" being manifested in your body?

Numbers 6:26 *The LORD lift up His countenance upon thee, and give thee peace.*

Keep on Serving...

Don't Fear the Fire!

Psalm 66:8-12 *O bless our God, ye people, and make the voice of his praise to be heard: Which holdeth our soul in life, and suffereth not our feet to be moved. For thou, O God, hast proved us: thou hast tried us, as silver is tried. Thou broughtest us into the net; thou laidst affliction upon our loins. Thou hast caused men to ride over our heads; we went through fire and through water: but thou broughtest us out into a wealthy place.*

Just to paraphrase a bit with Hebrew meanings: God holds our very life and keeps us steady in the fire. I see here that God desires, on occasion, to bring me into a net, a strong place or place of capture, and puts pressure on the small of my back and causes men to shake me and finally to go through fire and water. Wow - what a deal!

That could literally knock someone over in devastation, grief, hopelessness, and hatred of God amongst many other things. But if we hold on to Him, the holder of our soul, the tester in this situation, it says He will bring us out into a wealthy place... a running over wealth!

You know we are always trying to get wealthy without work. It's kind of like wanting to lose weight without cutting back and exercising. It very typically just doesn't happen. We may have been praying for provision or healing or spiritual growth; but instead of enduring through the fire of God's work, we run the other way. I will always be grateful for the fire God put me through, even if I seemed to have lost so much. God did a deep and profound work in me that I would never have experienced in the day to day. I am grateful to have seen the power of God's love and grace in such a devastating situation. I simply would not let Him go... I couldn't!!

Keep Walking...

If we will trust Him in the fire, our wealth is getting ready to explode.

Fire burns up the dross (our flesh) and purifies the precious person God created us to be in the first place.

Don't fear the fire!

Keep walking... forward... with Him... through the fire

Enjoy this song to help you survive the flesh fry and welcome in your wealth!

(Song by Jason Crabb)

No Resurrection Without a Death

I pray your spring is springing and your heart is hopeful during this resurrection season.

Many of you have heard my testimony of several years before I lost my sons. God specifically spoke to me after learning about a tragic death of someone in our church. His words were simple and life shaking. He simply said, "In death there is always a benefit." Trust me that is not what you want to hear when you have just gotten news of a tragic death. But I knew beyond the shadow of doubt that God had spoken. It was powerful, although my answer back to Him was, "God this is not the time for that." It did provoke me to begin searching the scriptures and of course when God speaks, it has already been written in His word.

Hebrews 9:16-17 *For where a testament is, there must also of necessity be the death of the testator. For a testament is of force after men are dead: otherwise it is of no strength at all while the testator liveth.*

I begin to realize whenever we let something "die" whether it be bitterness, fear, a dream that didn't come true, an old relationship, etc., that then, and only then can we have a testimony to share with others to give them hope. I remember in my many past twelve step meetings, that we would get up there and testify that we had been_____ (fill in the blank) for so many days. Everyone would clap and be encouraged that they could move forward and let their past habits "die" as well. It gave everyone hope.

We all need to let some things die so we can have new life, new hope, new dreams. There is no resurrection without a death.

Keep Walking...

There is no benefit from a last will and testament without a death. It is simply not available to you yet.

My ultimate message today, is that yes we can and should let some things die, so we can have new life and testify to encourage others. But, the greatest death was that of Jesus. Only after death, could His "last will and testament - the new covenant" be in effect. And it wasn't a benefit for a few, it was and is a benefit for everyone that will believe. In death there is a benefit and I hope you will receive and take part of every aspect of His "will" that you would grow, prosper and be a testimony of the life, death and resurrection of Jesus Christ.

I know you are busy, but I would ask that you take a few quiet minutes, now or later, and really listen to the song below.

There is no resurrection without a death. In death, there is always a benefit. Ponder the death and resurrection of Jesus.

Keep Dying...

(Song - This Blood - Lyrics by Rita Springer - performed by Prestonwood Baptist Church (www.youtube.com/watch?v=DQLlW_Bl4BA.)

Keep Walking..

WHY ARE YOU SO SAD?

Luke 24:25-26 *Then he said unto them, O fools, and slow of heart to believe all that the prophets have spoken: Ought not Christ to have suffered these things, and to enter into his glory?*

We have the previous scriptures in this chapter describing the disciples wandering down the road to Emmaus all bummed out about their King, their Savior, their Deliverer Who was crucified and hanging dead on a cross. I love and am deeply moved at the question Jesus asked them as He wanders with them unbeknownst to them. He simply asked them, "Why are you so sad?"

Can you imagine? He was the one who had taken on the whole sin of the world. He was beaten and bloodied beyond recognition and He is asking them why are they so sad? No matter what circumstance you are in, take a minute and allow Jesus to ask you, "Why are you so sad?" I promise it will change you!

Let's go back to the verses above. He calls them fools and unbelievers of all that He had taught them in the past few years. They simply didn't, and wouldn't hear what He had to say about His sufferings and death. They didn't understand it, so they ignored it. How often do we do that when God tries to speak to us? We don't like what He has to say; maybe it doesn't fit the outcome we want; we say it is the devil or ignore it and go ahead and do our own thing, or worse, simply stop believing. Somehow we don't accept that everything He has for us is the absolute very best, even though in the natural it might not look that way.

Notes in the Dake's Bible describe the above scriptures as follows: "Jews were good at believing the glory and the greatness of the kingdom that would make them great in the eyes of the Gentiles, but they would not be-

Keep Walking...

lieve prophecies of the humility and sufferings." Can we accept that our sufferings may be part of God's plan for our life, for ourselves and others? We often pray for God to mold us into His image, and when He does, we fight it with everything in us, even to the point that we don't believe it is Him and try to "cast it out."

If we do allow Jesus to work in the midst of our suffering, believe in His plan even though we may not like it, He might just change us to be more like Him. He will then send you to help someone else.

Blessed, broken and given away. We are blessed if we are in Him, we will be broken and the question remains, will we allow Him to create a powerful testimony of His great work in us to be given away? I hope so.

Philippians 1:12 *But I would ye should understand, brethren, that the things which happened unto me have fallen out rather unto the furtherance of the gospel;*

Keep believing...

Forgetting Your Misery

I am grateful to remember our veterans today who make it possible for me to even write this message and send it out into the airwaves. The topic today is "forgetting your misery." I can't think of a better topic for our veterans and active duty military.

Job 11:13-18 *If thou prepare thine heart, and stretch out thine hands toward him; If iniquity be in thine hand, put it far away, and let not wickedness dwell in thy tabernacles. For then shalt thou lift up thy face without spot; yea, thou shalt be stedfast, and shalt not fear: Because thou shalt forget thy misery, and remember it as waters that pass away: And thine age shall be clearer than the noonday; thou shalt shine forth, thou shalt be as the morning. And thou shalt be secure, because there is hope; yea, thou shalt dig about thee, and thou shalt take thy rest in safety.*

I would simply like to put this into some practical steps or really just a simple language for today:

- Prepare your heart and stretch out your hands toward the only One who can really help you.
- Resist evil whether it be memories, bad habits, anti-Christ (anything opposite of Jesus) thoughts, words and actions. Especially resist those thoughts that are such vivid pictures that the enemy wants you to remember. Choose to think on things that are worthy and good and joyful and hopeful.

Philippians 4:8 *Finally, brethren, whatsoever things are true, whatsoever things are honest, whatsoever things are just, whatsoever things are pure, whatsoever things are lovely, whatsoever things are of good report; if there be any virtue, and if there be any praise, think on these things.*

Keep Walking...

- Then, and only then, can you lift up your face without sinful shame to the One who forgives all, even those sins that were purposed and intentional and designed to destroy and devastate ourselves and others. God gets the greatest glory when we forgive... it was how the love gift was intended.

- At this point, we "shall be" steadfast which in the Hebrew language means to be poured out and placed firmly and "shall" not fear. Sounds pretty stable to me and isn't that what we are all really after?

- In verse 16, it states that because of the previous information, you will forget your misery and only remember it as waters passing away; that your present time in life shall be clear and bright, though you were in a dark time, you would be like the brightest time of the day. That you would be secure because there is hope, and you can dig about and rest in safety. I so get the image of how our dogs (definitely plural) dig a little, circle around and then plop down totally secure and content (to wait for the next treat or excitement!)

I ask you if you are going through a tough time or just trying to draw closer to God, to literally walk yourself through the above steps, first and foremost, take those arms and streeeeeeetch towards God with a prepared heart. Did you know that research shows that when you lift up your head and arms, that your body chemistry changes. Maybe God knew that... ya think???

Keep stretching...

NEEDY DOGS

Good morning to you all. I was struck by something that I needed to be struck by this morning! From Oswald Chambers' devotional book, I quote the following:

"We all have moments when we feel better than ever before, and we say, "I feel fit for anything; if only I could always be like this!" We are not meant to be. Those moments are moments of insight which we have to live up to even when we do not feel like it. Many of are no good for the everyday world when we are not on the mountain top. Yet we must bring our everyday life up to the standard revealed to us on the mountain top when we were there."

I have to say, I really like my life when there is little stress. It seems as if God and I have this thing called life all figured out. And then.... I end up with seven needy dogs. I am stressed. I am mad about the small puppy dumped out of a speeding car that has a broken leg and peed on the floor. I want the other "visiting" dogs to lay on the floor and not move and be quiet so I don't get stressed out. I forget my years of prayers for our veterans and wounded warriors and "whatever I can do to make a difference" in their life prayers.

One dog's owner is a medic who saw devastation after devastation in Afghanistan. The first dog he had was not the right fit for a veteran with PTSD and had to be returned. Another had brain tumors and other health problems and needs us to keep his beloved pet while he goes through treatments. What happened to the mountain top prayer for these guys?

I need to, as Chambers says, bring my everyday life up to the standard, and my standard is God's will for me and answering my prayer with seven needy dogs. We pray and pray and pray and then God answers and we

Keep Walking...

don't like His ways. This morning, I realized my attitude and prayers needed changing. I began to thank God for His provisions enabling us to provide for these dogs... food, water (free artesian well water at that!), and dog training skills. I also thanked Him for my strong walking legs and my joy in walking, despite every dog wanting a turn to go with me every time, and oh so many kennels, indoors and out.

I write this with all of the dogs quietly sleeping in their different quarters. One beside my chair, the puppy curled up with his nasty smelling cast on my bedspread which happens to be on the floor, three downstairs, and the two Great Danes in their garage condo. Meanwhile, there are two veterans struggling for their physical, emotional and spiritual life waiting for these dogs to be their best friends.

1 Timothy 6:8 *And having food and raiment let us be therewith content.*

Hebrews 13:5 *Let your conversation be without covetousness; and be content with such things as ye have: for he hath said, I will never leave thee, nor forsake thee.*

Philippians 4:11 *Not that I speak in respect of want: for I have learned, in whatsoever state I am, therewith to be content.*

Oh that I would let these scriptures remind me. I have good food and clothing and I have a living God right here with me. Why would I not be content with the Creator of the Universe, the Sovereign, Omniscient, Omnipresent, Almighty God and seven lazy dogs?

And one more time:

Psalm 61:2 *From the end of the earth will I cry unto thee, when my heart is over-whelmed: lead me to the rock that is higher than I.*

Keep an attitude of gratitude.

Keep Walking..

JUST SITUATIONS

I want to focus on "situations." It is probably one of my favorite things to teach that God has shown me. We all have situations. Some are great, some are awful, some are confusing, some are horrific and traumatizing and some just are. But they all have one thing in common and that is that they are *just* situations. Situations are defined as your "condition; state of affairs."

1 John 4:18 *There is no fear in love; but perfect love casteth out fear: because fear hath torment. He that feareth is not made perfect in love.*

Some people seem to make it through a situation with their heads up and senses intact, while others fall to the pit of despair, hopelessness, worry and anxiety. God showed me the above scripture, that we all have situations, but it is the fear that torments us in it if we allow it. The crazy thing is, that if you are a believer, then fear is defeated because sin is defeated and "anything not of faith is sin." (**Romans 14:23**).

I love what E. Stanley Jones says in his devotional:

"The man who fights life's battles without fear, fights one enemy - the real thing confronting him. But the man who fights with fear within him, fights three enemies --the real thing to fight, plus the imaginary things built up by fear, plus the fear itself. And the greatest of these is fear."

God says His perfect love casts out fear, so why do we participate with it? Answer—because we don't trust God. We question God's character, integrity, goodness, assurance of safety and His greatest plan for our lives. Fear walks in self-effort and self-will trying to "handle" the situation.

Keep Walking...

Fear rules and torments because we don't rest in the fact that "perfect Love casts out all fear."

Colossians 2:14-15 *Blotting out the handwriting of ordinances that was against us, which was contrary to us, and took it out of the way, nailing it to his cross; And having spoiled principalities and powers, he made a shew of them openly, triumphing over them in it.*

Do you see this in your situation? He took fear (out of His perfect love for us), spoiled fear, and made an open show of triumph for all to see. So you see, without fear, it is just a situation and nothing more. The question is, are you tormented in your situation? When you are tormented it is hard to handle anything. Situations are life, but God can and will deliver you from fear. I mean... He already has!

Don't allow fear in your situation, just deal with the situation, and leave the torment behind. That is God's plan for your life. You can be assured it is a plan you can't even imagine. A better plan than you could ever do in your own self effort. Guaranteed!

Keep saying no to fear and yes to God.

Keep Walking..

God in Every Moment

What a busy time of the year. We tend to be stretched to the limits with school ending, baseball tournaments, graduations, marriages, gardening, lawn care and on and on. We need to focus on not getting overwhelmed and more importantly (this is for me), enjoying each task instead of rapidly checking them off to get to the next one on the list. God is in every moment, and every situation, so get in touch with Him in the most mundane of activities on the list and you will find your life to have so much more joy!

One of my friend's favorite scripture to meditate on when she feels rushed and overwhelmed is:

Psalm 31:15: *My times are in thy hand: deliver me from the hand of mine enemies, and from them that persecute me.*

Let your time be in His capable hands!

Keep Walking...

Being an Overcomer

Onto the topic which happens to be on overcoming. I have been studying the first three chapters of Revelation and what I noticed the most is what Jesus is really speaking to the churches. He tells them all the great things they have been doing, chastises them for the disobedient things and then always ends with "he that over cometh shall..." He seems to be saying that the most important thing, is not all the Christ like things you are doing, nor your crazy anti-Christ things, but instead that you are overcoming!

Revelation 2:10-11 *Fear none of those things which thou shalt suffer: behold, the devil shall cast some of you into prison, that ye may be tried; and ye shall have tribulation ten days: be thou faithful unto death, and I will give thee a crown of life. He that hath an ear, let him hear what the Spirit saith unto the churches; He that overcometh shall not be hurt of the second death.*

I love the above scripture because it tells me that Jesus know exactly how long my trial will be. For some in the church of Smyrna it was a 10 day period. He goes on to say, that if we are faithful, never doubting God's perfect way, that we will get the sought after crown of life.

Oswald Chambers says, "Our circumstances are the means God uses to exhibit just how wonderfully perfect and extraordinarily pure His Son is. Discovering a new way of manifesting the Son of God should make our heart beat with renewed excitement."

If God puts you into adversity, He is certainly able to supply all your needs (Philippians 4:19), and as the verse below says, *"that the life of Jesus also may be manifested in our body."*

Keep Walking..

2 Corinthians 4:10 *Always bearing about in the body the dying of the Lord Jesus, that the life also of Jesus might be made manifest in our body.*

The other thing that dogs us (an important word for us, haha!) is the fear that enters in to try to destroy the work of God in our situation. We take on fear of death, fear of trials, fear of abandonment, fear of failure and even fear of success. Why??? Jesus cared little about success or failure. E. Stanley Jones so eloquently reminds us that the story of Jesus is a story of apparent failure. We have to realize a faith that has a cross or an instrument of apparent death as its center cannot be a faith that worships success.

We don't have to succeed in doing it all right. (Read Revelation 2:10 again or chapters 1-3). We only have to be true to the Sovereign God, trust in His perfect ways, lean into Him with all we have, rest in His finished works and consider trials and tribulations as ways God uses to manifest His glory through us. Sounds like a lot, but all it really requires of us is believing and receiving Him, His grace and His love and greatest plan for our life. God's got this!

1 John 5:4-5 *For whatsoever is born of God overcometh the world: and this is the victory that overcometh the world, even our faith. Who is he that overcometh the world, but he that believeth that Jesus is the Son of God?*

Invite the fullness of Jesus into your next situation or trial as a welcome guest, no matter the severity. You might just be surprised.

Keep walking, Keep walking,

LOOK FOR THE TEACHER

I sometimes wonder if I ever will get tired of the topic of trusting God in adversity. I came across yet more scriptures that remind me of how God is IN every situation if we look for Him. He was in the Hebrew boys fire, He was totally involved in Job's situation, and let's not forget the devastating crucifixion of God's own Son—Jesus. He was smack dab in the middle of them all and each one of these people kept their focus on Him and came out on the other side. We can too!!

Isaiah 30:20-23 *[20]And though the Lord give you the bread of adversity, and the water of affliction, yet shall not thy teachers be removed into a corner any more, but thine eyes shall see thy teachers: [21]And thine ears shall hear a word behind thee, saying, This is the way, walk ye in it, when ye turn to the right hand, and when ye turn to the left. [22]Ye shall defile also the covering of thy graven images of silver, and the ornament of thy molten images of gold: thou shalt cast them away as a menstruous cloth; thou shalt say unto it, Get thee hence. [23]Then shall he give the rain of thy seed, that thou shalt sow the ground withal; and bread of the increase of the earth, and it shall be fat and plenteous: in that day shall thy cattle feed in large pastures.*

I love the amplified version of verse 20:

"And though the Lord gives you the bread of affliction, yet your Teacher will not hide Himself any more, but your eyes will constantly behold your Teacher."

So the Lord allows the adversity and affliction for a purpose. He wants us to use our spiritual eyes and ears to hear Him and turn away from idols. We so often depend on man, created things or our own good works to find our direction in life. He calls them idols and tells us to throw them away like a menstruous cloth. Verse 23 starts with "then" and the rest of the chapter shares

Keep Walking..

the fullness and abundance of what He will do for us. I encourage you to read all of Isaiah 30.

If you are stuck in any situation, I would like to make a suggestion that I assure you will change your life. Take one week (for starters) or even one day and "throw away" everything you turn to for help except Him. Remove all distractions and focus on the One who came to earth to show us how to walk in fullness. He will teach you to recognize His voice in every situation. Look for the Teacher in your worst trial. He's there I promise. Let Him use you and mold you in the situation, because you trust Him—not how fast you can get your own self out of the trial so you can pat yourself on the back because you "made it."

If you allow Him to do His deepest work in every detail of the trial, He will get the glory, you will be changed and many others will benefit from watching you and seeing the countenance of God in your life.

Meanwhile, you might just end up with large pastures for your cattle and lots of bread (vs. 23)!

Keep allowing Him...

Nothing Left to Eat

Good day to you all. I continue to glean such wisdom from Job and wanted to share how trying to be in control of your life, striving for self-sufficiency is a fruitless, vain existence and does nothing to glorify God—only self.

Job 20:20-22 from the NKJV seems to say it best for me: *Because he knows no quietness in his heart, He will not save anything he desires. Nothing is left for him to eat; therefore his well-being will not last. In his self-sufficiency he will be in distress; Every hand of misery will come against him.*

I struggle on occasion with this. Your heart just seems to be missing the peace of God that should rule and reign all the time. Instead you "consume" everything in front of you, trying to do more and more and as it says, there comes an endpoint—nothing left to eat or consume. And then you quickly come to a screeching, albeit humble halt, when you realize in your own strength, your peace, or should I say the peace of the Lord that lives within us, will "die" a quick early death. As the NKJV says, every hand of misery will come against us.

I love the book of Ecclesiastes. It is a whole book by Solomon trying to prove that you could live this life without God. He came to a big conclusion, that is wasn't possible.

Ecclesiastes 1:13-14 *And I gave my heart to seek and search out by wisdom concerning all things that are done under heaven: this sore travail hath God given to the sons of man to be exercised therewith. I have seen all the works that are done under the sun; and, behold, all is vanity and vexation of spirit.*

He tried everything to find happiness without God; wine, houses, vineyards, gardens, orchards, water pools,

Keep Walking..

servants, gold and silver, singers, musical instruments and it says he became great. His problem came from what "he" was able to do, not depending on God at all.

Ecclesiastes 2:10-12 *And whatsoever mine eyes desired I kept not from them, I withheld not my heart from any joy; for my heart rejoiced in all my labour: and this was my portion of all my labour. Then I looked on all the works that my hands had wrought, and on the labour that I had laboured to do: and, behold, all was vanity and vexation of spirit, and there was no profit under the sun.*

Job describes **Ecclesiastes 2:10-12** in chapter 20. Finally Solomon realized what Job had already figured out. The last verse in the book is well worth tucking deep down into your heart.

Ecclesiastes 12:13-14 *Let us hear the conclusion of the whole matter: Fear God, and keep his commandments: for this is the whole duty of man. For God shall bring every work into judgment, with every secret thing, whether it be good, or whether it be evil.*

Take a minute and think about what you are doing. Is it you doing everything in your own strength? Is it you trying to consume everything you can get your hands on? Is it you trying to "be" someone that God never intended or planned? Allow God into every area of your life. His identity working through you, His strength carrying you through everything He has called you to do. And finally, let His peace be ruling and reigning in your heart always.

You might find that "misery and distress" that Job talked about will be far from you!

Keep Walking...

Thank You?

I wonder how many times we have done something for someone and gotten aggravated that the person did not thank us or didn't pay us back, we didn't get a thank you card or any other form of acknowledgment. I know for me, I have been guilty of criticizing their poor manners, thinking, that that's the last time I'll help them out, or I'll never be willing to share another meal, another dollar or even another kind word with them. Often we may cover up with a "Christianese smile" or something, but the truth is, we don't understand why they couldn't part with a simple "thank you."

We have to step back and wonder why we did what we did in the first place. If we did it to get appreciation, a pat on the back, or just to show our Christian kindness—it was the wrong motive.

Matthew 6:2-4 *²Therefore when thou doest thine alms, do not sound a trumpet before thee, as the hypocrites do in the synagogues and in the streets, that they may have glory of men. Verily I say unto you, They have their reward. ³But when thou doest alms, let not thy left hand know what thy right hand doeth: ⁴That thine alms may be in secret: and thy Father which seeth in secret himself shall reward thee openly.*

Whether we admit it or not, we are all guilty of this. I have found the answer in the above scripture. If I do something nice or helpful and expect to get a thank you, an accolade, a gift or whatever, then that is my reward... period. If I do it as unto the Lord, without any expectations other than pleasing Him and bringing Him delight, then verse 4 says God will reward me openly.

So here's the question: Would you rather have man reward you or God? I guarantee that God has the greater reward. When we do things as "unto the Lord," we

Keep Walking..

resist participating with that "life is all about me" attitude which results in making ourselves feel good, needed and worthy. We are also able to forgive those who have not provided the accolades we had hoped for, we resist judging them, and hopefully, we pray for them.

Colossians 3:23-24 *And whatsoever ye do, do it heartily, as to the Lord, and not unto men; Knowing that of the Lord ye shall receive the reward of the inheritance: for ye serve the Lord Christ.*

Next time the urge to feel hurt arises when someone doesn't thank you after you provided a kind thought or deed, rejoice, and again I say rejoice that this is a wonderful opportunity for God to reward you. I promise this really messes with the devil—totally not what he was plotting!

Keep forgiving...

The Spirituality of 50 Chiggers

I want to share the gist of something that E. Stanley Jones writes about. He states, "I get more of an understanding about how important it is to keep Jesus at the center of our lives and how He created us to do just that. When we veer away from that, disorder occurs."

I have had an intense, personal experience with this "focusing" during the past week. I was fortunate enough to get bitten by at least 50 chiggers from my shoulders to the ends of my feet! I say fortunate as I write this newsletter because it very much showed me this spiritual principle. I have focused on these chiggers like you can't imagine, and I must say they have provided physical and spiritual torment. Why spiritual? Because they are all I can think about. I can't hardly get a prayer up to God, without going back to the itchy, burning torment of these bites. I remind myself that these are just chiggers that will go away in a week. I think about my brothers and sisters that fight torment in so many ways that probably won't go away in a week. It brings me compassion for them and for a minute gets my mind off me and my chigger friends.

It is important to remind ourselves that whatever we place our attention on grows. That can be great or it can be devastating physically, emotionally and spiritually. Whatever gets our attention, gets us! If you give self your primary attention, self will be drawn to the center of your focus and everything else then has to arrange around "self."

Psalm 77:11-13 *I will remember the works of the LORD: surely I will remember thy wonders of old. I will meditate also of all thy work, and talk of thy doings. Thy way, O God, is in the sanctuary: who is so great a God as our God?*

Keep Walking..

E. Stanley Jones puts it like this, "For to have self at the center is to have a cancer at the center, because cancer cells are cells that make other cells contribute to them, instead of making themselves contribute to other cells." Wow, that is profound and I don't like it!!!!

Jesus came to serve not be served; He contributed to us all in a way we can hardly receive or contain. It's His arrangement to be God focused. He was able to endure the cross because of that focus. When we "arrange" ourselves around God instead of ourselves or our circumstances, He makes a way and it is a way that brings healing, provision and peace.

John 15:10 *If ye keep my commandments, ye shall abide in my love; even as I have kept my Father's commandments, and abide in his love.*

The few moments I have gotten my mind off these chiggers shows me how well this principle works. Don't be a cancer cell in life, making everyone contribute to you. Instead walk in God's plan, and contribute to others around you bringing you and them in health!

Keep focusing on Him...

When Helping Hurts

I want to try and share my heart on missions. Some of my thinking comes from a book that stimulated my thoughts and then, of course, the best is what Jesus Himself said in the Bible. The title of the book is "When Helping Hurts."

Often we are very excited to go on our first or #____ mission trip (you fill in the number). We are so full of godliness to help the poor and that is certainly a great thing. We do however have to be very careful that we don't see ourselves as the ones who have everything they need and are simply there to be the providers of that; food, love, ministry, toys, etc. The thought that "we" have everything and "they" have nothing is not biblical and that is "when helping hurts." A great, current example is how we have provided so much through government handouts, that we have created a crippled society that doesn't work which is definitely not biblical.

2 Thessalonians 3:10-12 *For even when we were with you, this we commanded you, that if any would not work, neither should he eat. For we hear that there are some which walk among you disorderly, working not at all, but are busybodies. Now them that are such we command and exhort by our Lord Jesus Christ, that with quietness they work, and eat their own bread.*

Instead there is a law of divine reciprocity.

Luke 6:38 *Give, and it shall be given unto you; good measure, pressed down, and shaken together, and running over, shall men give into your bosom. For with the same measure that ye mete withal it shall be measured to you again.*

There are so many messages here, but I want to try and focus on how this applies in missions. God's law of divine reciprocity is that when you give, God gives in return. When you plant a seed, you get a harvest When you put money in the bank, the bank returns interest. That is a reciprocal relationship. Giving and receiving belong together! Only when we give, are we in a position to expect to reach out and receive a harvest. If we are fortunate to go on a mission trip, it is NOT that we came to minister to the poor with all we have and 50 people got saved. That might happen and it is a good thing, if we remember it is the Spirit of God that saves and not us! But that should not be the total focus.

My focus is this: Can we go and give and expect to receive something individually from God and from others, no matter how poor or needy they seem? Others, even the most poor, have something to give as well. So often we miss it because we think we are the (okay forgive me here I go) "great, mighty, spiritual Christians with money, love, food, the Gospel" and they have nothing. They have a lot—if we would humble ourselves, listen, pay attention and allow them to give back the gifting God has given them..

We give as to God, and we receive as from God; but we should remain sensitive to the different ways in which God may deliver our harvest. It has been said that a miracle is either coming toward you or going past you all the time. Reach out and take it! Do not let it pass by!

I'll never forget when we went to Nicaragua and the people were so grateful that we came to help them. They invited us with their big beautiful smiles, into their homes, which happened to be sticks with plastic draped over them. That is what they had to give and they were sharing it to the fullest. How awful it would have been if we didn't go in and receive the "mite" that they offered... all that they had.

Mark 12:44 *For all they did cast in of their abundance; but she of her want did cast in all that she had, even all her living. ...And God was well pleased!*

Give in missions, all that you have, but don't forget to receive the harvest! Everyone has something to give in abundance. Look for it and receive it. Don't limit all that God has for you because you think someone doesn't have anything.

Keep giving, keep receiving.

Your Hardest Workout

Greetings to you! I am going to get right to the point today as I am feeling like any fluff needs to be set aside in this day and time. Many of us feel like everything is coming against us. Our thoughts about the future of this country, our thoughts about what our children and grandchildren are going to face in school, jobs, health care and the government of this nation. It is truly crazy, but then Jesus said it would be. I pray for an anointed and appointed by God, future president and government for one last revival in this country. But I am reminded that Jesus said :

Mark 13:8 *For nation shall rise against nation, and kingdom against kingdom: and there shall be earthquakes in divers places, and there shall be famines and troubles: these are the beginnings of sorrows.*

Perhaps a more evil leader shall arise and with that we shouldn't be surprised. Despite that thought, I continue to pray.

I was reading today and realized that as always, the Word can bring a hope and comfort when everything around you says Satan will win the battle. The battle might be the state of this nation, it might be your health, your family relationships, your job or whatever you feel that is falling apart. I am reminded of the last day of the life of Jesus. Get in the picture if you will.

There is a plot brewing to kill Jesus. We have the scene of the Last Supper where Jesus tells them that one of them will betray Him. Then He tells them to eat of His body and drink of His Blood. He then tells them that when He is raised again He will see them in Galilee. Lastly He tells Peter that he is going to betray Him not once, but three times. That's a lot to take in an afternoon!

Keep Walking...

Let's now look at a very important verse that we need to have planted in our hearts:

Luke 22:31-32 *And the Lord said, Simon, Simon, behold, Satan hath desired to have you, that he may sift you as wheat: But I have prayed for thee, that thy faith fail not: and when thou art converted, strengthen thy brethren.*

So often, we ask people to pray for us during our difficulties as we should. When people ask me I always say, "You need the prayers and I need the practice!" What is so important to see here is that Jesus says that He knows satan is sifting him/us like wheat, but that He has ALREADY prayed for him/us!! What exactly does He pray? That our faith doesn't fail! Jesus didn't pray for Peter to be delivered. He was praying something that would be far more beneficial for Peter—increased faith that would last a lifetime and bring great rewards. Our faith is up to us, not Him.

Faith has to be exercised like pressing through the hardest workout to get through. When we do that, we will be converted. If you look up the word converted in the dictionary it means to "To change; to transform; to apply or adapt to a new purpose; to become changed in character." Jesus is praying that we will cling to our faith, our hope in Him, and that we stick to it like finishing a race and not giving up. He will then adapt us to a new purpose, with a new character so that we can go and strengthen others.

Romans 5:2 *By whom also we have access by faith into this grace wherein we stand, and rejoice in hope of the glory of God.*

Faith is up to us and God responds with His grace. Our faith, His grace. Prayer is an act of faith by which we then have access to His grace. Our prayer, our faith, is an activation in us, to appropriate something Jesus has already accomplished, finished, done, completed.

Keep Walking..

He just wants to give it to us! He has done so much; He has done it all and yet all He asks of us is to believe and receive it. What a great deal for us! Whatever battle you are in, know that Jesus has already prayed for you, not to get out of the situation, but to press through so that He can use you for a new purpose. Don't hate the fire. Open your eyes and find Jesus in the fire doing a beautiful work.

Keep faithful...

Called Out of Darkness

Good morning to you all. It is a bit cooler, meaning 88 less humid degrees here, and after the rain we finally received, it is bright and beautiful. However, it is not nearly as precious as His light.

I remember some very dark days of depression in my teenage and early college years. I tried diluting them (yes, I drank heavily), getting an abundant supply of pills from the university psychiatrist, and even some good things like running, and swimming. Basically, anything I could do to not feel the depression. In other words, "chemical happiness," which worked for a moment until it wore off. It was an endless pursuit, a full-time job if you will.

I remember after years of twelve step programs, still feeling the depression and darkness and really never knowing what joy felt like in its truest sense. If you have never experienced joy, you don't have any idea what it is like or know what you are missing. Then I found hope in a church that preached the Word and the Word alone. I had grown up in religion, but trust me religion does not introduce you to joy!! It was when I was taught to read the Word and scriptures that they began to mean something to me—I began to believe and receive anything that Jesus had to offer me.

Psalm 36:9 *For with You is the fountain of life: in Your light shall we see light.* (NKJV)

The fountain of life is not in my career, or my nice family, my good manners, my donations to charity or my church work, it is with Him. I began to believe in this man Jesus who came to walk this earth and who encountered the deepest and darkest situations that we all might have to face. He did it and said, that if you know me, then I will show you how to do it as well. Follow me. I had tried everything else and nothing else worked.

In the scripture above it says in God's light we shall see light. I can't see light and hope and joy without Him. No wonder I never had it before.

1 Peter 2:9 *But ye are a chosen generation, a royal priesthood, an holy nation, a peculiar people; that ye should shew forth the praises of him who hath called you out of darkness into his marvelous light:*

He has called us out of darkness into His marvelous light. Can we hear His voice? He is always calling us.

John 10:27-28 *My sheep hear my voice, and I know them, and they follow me: And I give unto them eternal life; and they shall never perish, neither shall any man pluck them out of my hand.*

I am blessed to be able to share the grace of God. He delivered me from depression, even when Satan came at me and tried to get me to go back into the darkness when both of my sons died tragic deaths. No way - I love dogs but I am not going back to vomit!!

Proverbs 26:11 *As a dog returneth to his vomit, so a fool returneth to his folly.*

Instead, I choose to stay in His marvelous light.

Keep walking...

LIFE UPSIDE DOWN

Just for a minute, I want us to look at how the world wants to deceive us. That everything is okay and we should not be offended by anything, or on the other hand offended by everything. It is a crazy world out there. Please keep your nose, your mind, your heart and every other part of you in the Word!!

Matthew 24:4-5 *And Jesus answered and said unto them, Take heed that no man deceive you. For many shall come in my name, saying, I am Christ; and shall deceive many.*

This song describes it perfectly. Take a minute to find it on YouTube: (Living Life Upside Down- Jason Crabb)

John has a new way of looking at life
He's tired of his job, his kids and his wife
Says the secret to his success
Was in leaving and finding himself
Now he's someone to somebody else

You say we've risen to a new age of truth
And you're calling it a spiritual Godly pursuit
But I say, but I say

[Chorus]
What if we've fallen to the bottom of a well
Thinking we've risen to the top of a mountain
What if we're knocking at the gates of hell
Thinking that we're heaven bound

Keep Walking..

And what if we spend our lives thinking of ourselves
When we should have been thinking of each other
What if we reach up and touch the ground
To find we're living life, upside down

We've got a program to saving the earth
While unborn children are denied their right to birth
One baby's blessed, another cursed
Have we made this world better or worse
Now the life of a tree comes first?

You say we've risen to a new age of light
You're telling me what used to be wrong is now right
But I say, I say

Isaiah 5:20 *Woe unto them that call evil good, and good evil; that put darkness for light, and light for darkness; that put bitter for sweet, and sweet for bitter!*

Keep walking...

Fruit Inspector

Good day to you all! I remember being in Bible school and being taught that our main goal in discerning someone's spirituality is to be a fruit inspector; not necessarily by the persons words and actions, but by the fruit they produced. I never forgot it. Today I was reading a very familiar passage.

John 15:5 *I am the vine, ye are the branches: He that abideth in me, and I in him, the same bringeth forth much fruit: for without me ye can do nothing.*

We often work very hard for God and wonder why things in our lives are not changing. Maybe we are not abiding. Abiding in the Greek language means "to stay." I am sure most of you abide sometimes and you probably may see some fruit. But then again we try to do things ourselves instead of "staying" with Jesus and the fruit dries up.

What if we could truly capture the full essence of "I in Him and He in me?" There is a real fullness in this, a richness, an abundance, an overflow... and I could go on and on about this statement. The words of Jesus promise that we will bring forth much fruit. Of course we would expect that because Jesus accomplished everything we need at the Cross.

We like to think we believe this scripture but then we are off trying to accomplish things on our own again; in other words we move away from our "coupling." We all know what happens in a marriage when husbands and wives do their own thing. There is no unity, no real strength, and no deep spiritual growth. There can't be because God tells us when we are married we become one. Marriage is an analogy of what being in Him means. If we truly understood the Gospel, we would get that. It would be normal because we would have been taught the

Keep Walking..

above scripture, we would abide intimately and produce much fruit. Instead we get two busy people doing a lot of stuff with no intimacy. Kind of like most people's relationship with Jesus.

Look back at the last part of the scripture. It says that without Him, we can do nothing!! I mean really?? You ought to see all the things I do... and He says I do nothing. You have to ask yourself—what does nothing mean? It means just that—you may do a lot of worldly things, but this is about spirituality. We will do nothing that represents the Father, Son and Holy Spirit. We will accomplish nothing that the two edged sword could do with one Word. We will not make a difference in anyone's life that has eternal value. We may get our Christian selves to heaven but end up in one of the smaller rooms!

And in case you missed it, Paul reminds us again:

2 Corinthians 3:5 *Not that we are sufficient of ourselves to think anything as of ourselves; but our sufficiency is of God;*

Are you thinking of yourself and your ability? This is a clear statement to stop. Instead I pray we will learn to abide more fully.

And lastly, I will conclude with a great statement from E. Stanley Jones. "God does not inflict any torture. The departure itself produces the torture. It is inherent." In my words, God is not the one causing a crop failure, it is your departure from Him. Why??? Cause the Word says so!!!

Keep abiding...

Keep Walking...

LIFE... SERIOUSLY?

Good morning to you all. I am grateful for spring springing!! I look out my window as I write and see blooming dogwoods and azaleas and sun. What a great combination!!

I write this message to myself. There has been way too much going on and I don't handle the multitudes of tasks as well as I used to. It seems like I get a bit overwhelmed because I am such a "completer." So I look to good old King Solomon to see how to not take this life so seriously.

Ecclesiastes 5:20 *For he shall not much remember the days of his life; because God answereth him in the joy of his heart.*

The amplified Bible says it like this:

For he shall not much remember (seriously) the days of his life, because God (Himself) answers and corresponds to the joy of his heart (the tranquility of God is mirrored in him)

Somehow that really speaks to me. If I can focus on joy, then God answers me and I don't fret about the things going on around me or the things that are undone. This Psalm also reminds me that even when I can't seem to remember to focus on anything, much less joy, that as a born again believer there is light in my own manufactured darkness.

Psalm 112:4 *Unto the upright there ariseth light in the darkness: he is gracious, and full of compassion, and righteous.*

I love the Hebrew words and if you would allow me to do a Mary Pat, Hebrew amplified version, it would look like this:

Keep Walking..

"For you my born again child, there irradiates and shoots forth beams of illumination and happiness in the misery, destruction, death, ignorance, sorrow and wickedness. You are gracious and full of compassion, and righteous in Me."

It is my own ignorance to get all overwhelmed with the useless or vain things of life. I am grateful that God looks beyond that and shoots those beams of happiness right though them. He is so merciful and His mercy never runs out!

Psalm 106:1 *Praise ye the LORD. O give thanks unto the LORD; for he is good: for his mercy endureth for ever.*

In looking up this scripture, I found that in the Bible there are 43 verses that say that God's mercy endures forever. I am glad I know this God and He knows me!

Keep looking up...

I'll Do What I Can't

I think spring is finally here!! When we enter into new seasons of our life, there are many things that may push us to stretch beyond our own skills, knowledge and physical, emotional and spiritual capacity.

Hebrews 11:8-10 *By faith Abraham, when he was called to go out into a place which he should after receive for an inheritance, obeyed; and he went out, not knowing whither he went. By faith he sojourned in the land of promise, as in a strange country, dwelling in tabernacles with Isaac and Jacob, the heirs with him of the same promise: For he looked for a city which hath foundations, whose builder and maker is God.*

The key words here to me are "not knowing" but by faith.

Hebrews 12:1-2 *¹Wherefore seeing we also are compassed about with so great a cloud of witnesses, let us lay aside every weight, and the sin which doth so easily beset us, and let us run with patience the race that is set before us, ²Looking unto Jesus the author and finisher of our faith; who for the joy that was set before him endured the cross, despising the shame, and is set down at the right hand of the throne of God.*

Look around and find your inspiration in people who are moving forward and laying aside all the weight of the world — "running" the race which is set before them. The truth is, we really don't know what is before us. Often we either try to get more knowledge and skill to deal with things up ahead, or we go into fear wondering how we will ever get through something. It could be as simple as a math test, a job interview or facing a huge giant in our lives. Regardless we depend on our own capacity or an evil spirit of fear to help us get through. Neither are really effective and both are designed to wear us out.

The above scriptures tell us to "look to the Builder and Maker" and look unto Jesus who endured and then sat down. He didn't look at his circumstances and surroundings but stayed focused on His Father. What if we really knew that our joy came after enduring our cross? If we could grab hold of that, anything we go through wouldn't seem nearly so bad. Instead, there would be an anticipation of what God was up to, to make our lives so much better.

Here is a scripture we often quote to get through tough times:

Philippians 4:13 *I can do all things through Christ which strengtheneth me.*

God has deposited everything in Christ and it is all I need and already mine. Something that is sticking in my mind right now, is the simple phrase, "I'll do what I can't... (but through Him, I can)."

Looking back at Hebrews 11, let me summarize my point today. It goes something like this: Faith... Go... Not Knowing... and finally finding the city which already has foundations (and I promise strong ones!) whose Builder and Maker is God!

Go do what you can't in Jesus name and you might just find yourself in a very nice spring season!!

Keep going...

Victory March

There is much power to be found when there is unity. We see that in the building of the Tower of Babel. Everyone was on the same page to build this big, idol tower and the only thing that could stop them was the full Trinity.

Genesis 11:4-7 *And they said, Go to, let us build us a city and a tower, whose top may reach unto heaven; and let us make us a name, lest we be scattered abroad upon the face of the whole earth. And the LORD came down to see the city and the tower, which the children of men builded. And the LORD said, Behold, the people is one, and they have all one language; and this they begin to do: and now nothing will be restrained from them, which they have imagined to do. Go to, let us go down, and there confound their language, that they may not understand one another's speech.*

We also see unity in godliness. In Acts, we see that when the church body was all in one accord, there was a huge outpouring of the Holy Spirit.

Acts 4:31 *And when they had prayed, the place was shaken where they were assembled together; and they were all filled with the Holy Ghost, and they spake the word of God with boldness.*

With the thought of the power of unity, I returned to an old teaching I had put together called "Victory March." It was a loving title of a ministry Rick and I had in the beginning days of salvation. Let me give you a quick outline and then I encourage you to study and meditate on this topic. It really is a powerful message.

Keep Walking..

Definitions:

Victory - the overcoming of an enemy, opponent, or any difficulty; a triumph.

March - to proceed with measured steps, advance steadily; onward progress.

Examples of a march: military marches, parades, a march at the Capitol for a cause. The ultimate march that represents all of the following characteristics was the march of Jericho (Joshua 6).

Characteristics of a march: 1) it is for the observation of others 2) if you are out of step, you don't stop, quit or turn around, but quickly get back in step with the group 3)obedience 4) submission 5) knowledge (of the mission either partial or complete 6) unity 7) practice a pre-planned goal (ultimately the plan Jesus has for our life) 8) group and self discipline- you stop and start only at the direction of the superior (a work of the Holy Spirit in our lives) 9) the people marching do not receive the credit, but the superior over them does (to God be the glory!)

In summary a "Victory March" is a group of people in unity, striving for a common goal of perfection which will be observed by others. That should be the goal of the church. Then and only then will people want to be a part of something so awesome - a life in Him!!

Remember where there is unity, there is power. Whether it be the church, your marriage, your family, your workplace, your neighborhood unity will allow God to do His greatest work!

The Trinity, a perfect form of a march in unity!

Keep marching victoriously...

The River Again

Rick and I had a wonderful time in Alaska. As always, it is good to be back home to our simple lifestyle. Being wined and dined and taken care of is good, but I still prefer working outside and getting dirt under my fingernails!

The vastness of Alaska was breath-taking. It exhibited the power of God and His hand upon the earth. The mountains, the ocean and especially the glaciers were a spectacular playground for beautiful wildlife.

On the other end of the spectrum is the devastation we find in the news such as the genocides, the suicides, the bombings, the terror that is rampant. This can be overwhelming if we don't stay focused on God's ultimate plan for our lives, and just to make sure you know, it is not about this life on earth as we know it. With that, I am so encouraged by this Psalm.

Psalm 46:1-4 *To the chief Musician for the sons of Korah, A Song upon Alamoth. God is our refuge and strength, a very present help in trouble. Therefore will not we fear, though the earth be removed, and though the mountains be carried into the midst of the sea; Though the waters thereof roar and be troubled, though the mountains shake with the swelling thereof. Selah. There is a river, the streams whereof shall make glad the city of God, the holy place of the tabernacles of the most High.*

I love the first verse simply because the word "present" jumps out at me. This passage is not just for those going through tough times thousands of years ago, but God being our very present help. That is right now and right where you will be every minute of every day.

Jump in this Psalm with me for a minute. The earth

is being annihilated, the mountains are crumbling down into the vast sea, the waters roar and are troubled (Hebrew - "fermented with scum") and there you are in the midst. What does God do? He tells you about a river. The river the writer is referring to, from his background, is the Nile river. The river, in its time, represented prosperity which is the Hebrew word for river. The Nile would swell up and much increase would come forth.

What God is saying is that no matter what is going on, if you will look away from the devastation and to Him, prosperity and increase will come. There is just something about that river...

Jump in...

Judgment and Singing

Satan uses our weaknesses to rear his ugly head. He wants to separate us from others, condemn us with our past and then try to destroy us. I always think of the analogy of a group of sheep. The ones hanging out with the herd and staying together have a strength. The weak or stubborn ones lag behind and they are the ones the fox can easily pick off. The moral of that story is stay in fellowship with other believers, even when things are tough. If the enemy can make you feel dirty, separate and not worthy, you can be sure he is coming in for the kill.

What we must always remember is that our strength and righteousness comes not from ourselves but Christ in us. That needs to be a daily reminder when the enemy comes to remind us of our past or our weak areas.

I was struck by the following Psalm the other day:

Psalm 54:1 *Save me, O God, by thy name, and judge me by thy strength.*

I am judged by God's strength, not mine!! I liken it to a big body builder who is super strong, and a 90 pound weakling. If that body builder is judging the 90 pounder by his (the body builder's) strength, then this small guy has nothing to worry about. The 90 pounder holds the secret of God's strength and defense, e.g., David and Goliath!

Psalm 59:9 *Because of his strength will I wait upon thee: for God is my defence.*

Again, it is God's strength that I wait on, not me, through self effort, defending myself. I just need to sit back and rest in Him and let Him work it out through me, not because of me! If I can do that, then the rest of Psalms 59 makes perfect sense.

Keep Walking..

Psalm 59:16-17 *But I will sing of thy power; yea, I will sing aloud of thy mercy in the morning: for thou hast been my defence and refuge in the day of my trouble. Unto thee, O my strength, will I sing: for God is my defence, and the God of my mercy.*

I am judged by God's strength and because of His strength, I will wait and because I am rested and brought through the trial, I have plenty of energy to sing!

Keep singing...

Keep Walking...

The Sight of Faith

I would like to share some thoughts sparked by a book recommended many years ago by my pastor in Florida, "Christ the Healer," by F. F. Bosworth. It has to do with "the sight of faith." I want to remind you that it is impossible to have faith with your eyes. It is the mind, not the optic nerve, that sees. For example; you cannot see your money in the bank with your eyes, but with your mind.

When you try to look "in faith" with your eyes, you will only succumb to depression and anxiety because you will only see in the natural. I don't care how great of a life you have, your senses will sooner or later bring fear, oppression and heaviness. Walking by faith is walking by sight of a better kind. Bosworth states, "Faith actually is the most rational thinking in the world, because it is based on the greatest of facts and realities. It sees God, it sees Calvary where disease and sin were canceled and it sees the promises of God and His faithfulness which are more certain than the foundations of a mountain. Faith sees the health and strength given on the cross as already belonging to us. Faith refuses to see anything but God and what He says."

Hebrews 11:23-31 *²³By faith Moses, when he was born, was hid three months of his parents, because they saw he was a proper child; and they were not afraid of the king's commandment. ²⁴By faith Moses, when he was come to years, refused to be called the son of Pharaoh's daughter; ²⁵Choosing rather to suffer affliction with the people of God, than to enjoy the pleasures of sin for a season; ²⁶Esteeming the reproach of Christ greater riches than the treasures in Egypt: for he had respect unto the recompence of the reward. ²⁷By faith he forsook Egypt, not fearing the wrath of the king: for he endured, as see-*

ing him who is invisible. ²⁸Through faith he kept the passover, and the sprinkling of blood, lest he that destroyed the firstborn should touch them. ²⁹By faith they passed through the Red sea as by dry land: which the Egyptians assaying to do were drowned. ³⁰By faith the walls of Jericho fell down, after they were compassed about seven days. ³¹By faith the harlot Rahab perished not with them that believed not, when she had received the spies with peace.

If you focus on the scriptures above you will get the picture of what it takes to walk in faith... the sight of faith. Let me see if I can sum it up.

If I am to walk in faith, I must not entertain any fear (vs 23). I must refuse to be called anything by the world's standards but rather rest in my identify with Christ (vs. 24). I have to personally make a choice to suffer as Christ did to obtain the promise rather than get involved in some "feel good" experience that deceives me and takes me into bondage (vs. 25). I have to trust in a greater reward that I cannot yet see (vs. 25-26). I must endure with that spiritual sight and "see" Him and His promises that for the moment are as invisible as He is (vs. 27). I must keep with the "rituals" of prayer, fellowship and study, even when it seems to be so dry and hopeless (vs. 28). I must pass through (keep walking!!) to get to the other side. In other words, no camping on the mountain top or in the valley, but a life moving for God (vs. 29). I must expect that the walls will fall down, when I have been around the same mountain oh so many times (vs. 30). Finally I must believe in peace... that would be the Prince of Peace, that has my back every time. Come to think of it, He has my front and my sides covered too!

Read all of Chapter 11 in Hebrews and do your own study of faith. It was never done with the optic nerve!!

Keep walking...

A Scriptural Picture

I would like to share something Rick said on the call that created the most visual picture in my mind. We had a question about performance and perfectionism; how we had to get everything done and do it in a Christian manner and how difficult that is. I am going to try to create this picture in your mind. Begin to imagine what this looks like from God's perspective which is really what faith is—seeing things from His Word.

Okay, I am ready to paint. We are Christians and we want to be "good" ones. In our hearts we would like God to rest on His throne while we perform for Him. "God, I have a situation and I am going to pray and read Your Word and I am going to make you real proud of me as Your daughter. Sit on Your throne and watch me! I hope you will see how much good I am doing for You. I am making decisions, I am feeding the homeless, I tithe and go to church and Sunday school and, and, and...I hope you are proud of me and wish you could reach out and pat me on the back and tell me how well I am doing!"

Sounds fairly good right? Well guess what? It is not scriptural. God says for us to rest in His finished work. He works and we rest, nothing like the picture above.

Hebrews 4:9-11 *There remaineth therefore a rest to the people of God. For he that is entered into his rest, he also hath ceased from his own works, as God did from his. Let us labour therefore to enter into that rest, lest any man fall after the same example of unbelief.*

Jesus never tried to figure things out; or what the next situation He would encounter would be; or what He would need to do. In other words, He didn't plan for weeks ahead how to feed 5000 or cast out a devil or toss tables in the temple. Instead He trusted His Father's

Keep Walking..

plan. He knew that He already had it all worked out, as it would need to be, for the greatest good for all. He knew that life was not His problem, but God's.

I have come to the conclusion that things in my life are not my problem. God purchased me, bought me with a price, and I agreed. That means I do what He tells me to do, and that includes the things above, but I focus on Him. That is what a slave/servant does. He just does what His Master tells him and doesn't try to figure out his own way. It really makes it much easier.

1 Corinthians 6:20 *For ye are bought with a price: therefore glorify God in your body, and in your spirit, which are God's.*

1 Corinthians 7:23 *Ye are bought with a price; be not ye the servants of men.*

John 12:26 *If any man serve me, let him follow me; and where I am, there shall also my servant be: if any man serve me, him will my Father honour.*

I so want God to honor me. He says to serve Him, not man; to rest in the finished work. He knows the beginning from the end and already has our lives worked out. God doesn't sleep or slumber, however He does require it of us! I think I will just rest and let Him stay up and watch over all my situations!

Psalm 121:3-4 *He will not suffer thy foot to be moved: he that keepeth thee will not slumber. Behold, he that keepeth Israel shall neither slumber nor sleep.*

Keep resting in Him...

Keep Walking...

KNOW ANYTHING?

Peaceful Christmas holidays to you all. Remember it was the Prince of Peace that was born. Anything less than that defeats the whole purpose of this special celebration time.

As we join together with family, (and some of them are tough family members to be around), God makes a profound statement that I think can benefit us - and the other person as well for that matter!

1 Corinthians 8:1-3 *Now as touching things offered unto idols, we know that we all have knowledge. Knowledge puffeth up, but charity edifieth. And if any man think that he knoweth anything, he knoweth nothing yet as he ought to know. But if any man love God, the same is known of him.*

Haven't we all had some knowledge to "help" some of those difficult family members? Maybe we have college degrees in a specific area, or have read a book or heard something on TV, or heaven forbid, we heard it preached and we think "they need to know this." So we seek them out at that family dinner and proceed to tell them all we know.

The scriptures above says if we know anything, we know nothing, unless the goal is out of complete, unadulterated love. We have to be very careful as to our motive in sharing with the person. Is it to make me look like I know a lot? Well then I am puffed up. Is it to make me feel like I am a spiritual giant and need to minister to someone? Then I "knoweth nothing as I ought to know" because it is more about me trying to be somebody—perhaps omniscient or all knowing. Only God is that.

What if we didn't try to fix them in some undercover, "spiritual" way and just love them? If we could set aside

Keep Walking..

all judgment, all things we want to say to "help" them and just hang out with them, I bet God might just show up.

Really meditate on the above scripture. Love edifies. The word edify in the Greek means a "house builder or construction." If we really look at the situation, I know that deep down, we just want to build the person up. Once again... "If any man think that he knoweth anything, he knoweth nothing." Ouch. On the other hand, if we can offer simple kindness, encouraging words and pleasant conversation, we might just get that house built after all!

Keep building...

No Sin - No Christmas

I hope everyone has the Prince of Peace in the forefront of their minds during the Christmas season. Remember if there was no sin, there would be no Christmas. Truly receive your forgiveness of all sin, past, present and future and live boldly in the grace of God. It is the best gift you could ever receive!

1 Kings 3:7 *And now, O LORD my God, thou hast made thy servant king instead of David my father: and I am but a little child: I know not how to go out or come in.*

I think this is an overwhelmingly awesome scripture for us to look at today. In a sense, it has a Christmas overtone to it. Jesus came as a crying baby vulnerable to all of the world's ways, but God had a perfect plan!

This passage has to do with Solomon who is praying for wisdom. He saw himself as too young, too inexperienced; but God saw him so differently. He calls us to carry out a purpose that He created in us from the beginning and is thus responsible for giving us everything we need to carry it out. Here we have Solomon who wants wisdom because he acknowledges that he is just a little child, barely knowing how to go out or come in. How many of us feel like that?

I think it is important to point out something. If we say we are nothing out of inferiority, then basically we have told God that His ways are not perfect which opposes scripture. It is out of humility that we can truly say that we are nothing because we are trusting in Him.

2 Samuel 22:31 *As for God, his way is perfect; the word of the LORD is tried: he is a buckler to all them that trust in him.*

That brings me to the book of Ecclesiastes that Solomon wrote. It has always been one of my favorite books be-

Keep Walking..

cause it seems as real today as it did then. The whole summary of this book is trying to do life without God. Solomon started out humble, asking only for wisdom, which God gave him liberally. He then tried to see if he could have the abundant life a number of other ways ---women, music, knowledge, stuff. The great thing is that he realized that no matter what you have, if you don't have God, life is not worth living. In the end, that truly is the most important thing to learn, no matter how hard the road it takes to get there.

So Lord, we cry out to you that we really are but little children, not knowing the steps to take or how to make that next decision. Give us wisdom, but most importantly, let us trust that we really don't have to know because we know YOU!

Proverbs 16:9 *A man's heart deviseth his way: but the LORD directeth his steps.*

Psalm 37:23 *The steps of a good man are ordered by the LORD: and he delighteth in his way.*

Sounds like God knows your way. Just follow Him... He's got this trip!!

Keep following.

Encouragement in the Prison

Good morning and blessings to you all. Thank you for all of the feedback on my confession about impatience! I am grateful that I have people out there who will share their experiences with me and give me truth without the sugar coating. It is good to see the Word that James expresses on confession in action.

James 5:16 *Confess your faults one to another, and pray one for another, that ye may be healed. The effectual fervent prayer of a righteous man availeth much.*

My intent was to "get it out in the airwaves" so that I could get feedback and have the Holy Spirit, the devil and whomever else wanted to hear that I was steadfastly going to overcome this thing. The Greek word "confess" means to acknowledge and that was certainly easy enough; the word "faults" means an unintentional or intentional side slip or falling away, and the word "healed" means cure. There you have it. I acknowledged my intentional and unintentional slips to you all and now the "curing" is coming. Thank you and I hope you will be free to confess your faults so that you may be healed as well. The WORD works!!

My lesson today comes from the book of Philippians which I will share from the Amplified Bible:

Philippians 1:12 *Now I want you to know and continue to rest assured, brethren, that what (has happened) to me (this imprisonment) has actually only served to advance and give a renewed impetus to the (spreading of the) good news (the Gospel).*

Paul is excited because he is not bowing down to fear or the world's way but is continuing to share the Gospel while in prison. He goes on to share in later verses that all the prison guards and inmates are see-

Keep Walking..

ing and hearing him as this "Christian man." Paul is thrilled because many are becoming more confident and bold to speak; and publish the Word of God with more freedom and indifference to the consequences. Some were "preaching Christ" out of a party spirit, but others out of a loyal spirit and goodwill. But here are Paul's words in verse 18: "But what does it matter, so long as either way, whether in pretense (for personal ends) or in all honesty (for the furtherance of the Truth), Christ is being proclaimed? And in that I (now) rejoice, yes, and I shall rejoice (hereafter) also."

How cool is that? He doesn't care how their motives impact the speaking of the Word; just that it is spoken aloud! The Bible says 'Faith comes by hearing and hearing by the Word of God (Romans 10:17)."

I have been reading from the information provided by the "Voice of the Martyrs" whereby the Communist government would print publications mocking the Word of God. The Christians were thrilled to get it because it contained the scriptures they were mocking!!! It was basically their "Bible" and meant the world to them because that is all they had. Makes me think of Genesis 50:20 that what was meant for harm, God turns to good!!

My heart in writing this newsletter was to encourage you in your prison. If you are in a seeming prison of relationship problems, financial woes, sorrow and devastation, traumatic news, sickness and disease or any number of things, I ask the question - can you look at it, as Paul did, as an opportunity to further the gospel? At the loss of my two sons, mother and sister, instead of devastation and despair, it has opened up the opportunity to share how God has and is bringing me through.

Isn't that just like God to bring fruit from that old, hard seed we were willing to "drop in the ground." Remember, a seed has to be planted before fruit can

Keep Walking...

come forth (John 12:24). I am so grateful that God didn't "hold tightly" to His only Son, but was willing to let Him die, only for fruit to come forth for eternity. Don't despair what you are going through... it may be a huge opportunity in disguise!!

Preach Christ Period!

INTERNAL WEAKNESS BRINGS EXTERNAL OPPOSITION

Peace and goodwill to all of you during this season that we have chosen to remember the birth of Jesus. Most importantly is remembering "Jesus is the reason," not just during the weeks of December, but each and every day. Every day we live is "Christmas;" every day we should be grateful for this Baby!!

This morning I was reading about King Solomon in **1 Kings 11:1-6**. Here we have the wisest man on earth whose heart began to be swayed by his desire of many women to become his wives. God warned him about not hanging out with all those pretty, heathen women but after a time, Solomon's own heart began to be drawn to other gods. The study notes in my Bible made a profound statement that got my attention. They said that, *"The greatest kingdom of the known world began to crumble not from external opposition, but from internal weakness."* That is a huge responsibility to take on for us as individuals. It is so much easier to say that others or the devil is attacking us.

Maybe it is those irritating people that are causing you to act the way you do; or you may have financial, marriage, health, or just plain old basic sin issues that cause you to be struggling as a child of God. Maybe, just maybe, it's not "out there," but "in here." We have to ask ourselves then, what is internal weakness? I simply believe that our thoughts are more about "out there" than "in Him- in here." Our minds have not been renewed so we become internally weak. Whatever we focus on, grows. That is a neurological fact. We must decide if our own troubles are of our own making.

In verses 14-25 of 1 Kings 11, we find that the Lord *"raised up an adversary against Solomon."*

Keep Walking...

We may say, "No, I think that God is good and the writer really meant that the devil begin to attack Solomon's kingdom." I used to think that way but now believe that if we look back at the book of Job, chapter one, we see that the devil always has to ask God for permission before he can do anything!!

In this passage, we see that in addition to the internal weakness, the Lord now brings external opposition by raising up adversaries. You may think this is cruel of God, but remember, more than anything, He wants to save us from our own self destruction and will unleash all of hell if it means bringing you back into a full, focused relationship with Him where the blessings can flow.

Let's put this in modern day terms. Perhaps your child has stopped studying and his grades are falling. That is the internal weakness. Now if mom and dad take away his privileges or ground him etc., then you are unleashing some external opposition, an adversary if you will, to bring him back to "righteousness." Are you evil or cruel? NO! You want the best for your child. God really does know what is best for us even though we don't see it.

The moral of the story is don't blame others quickly, recognize your weaknesses and ask God to help. Otherwise He might have to resort to other methods that could have easily been by-passed had we only trusted that "Father knows best!"

Look inward always...

FAITHFUL

Last week we had a big discussion on whether difficult things happening around us are God events or devil events. I am not convinced any of us ever know for sure so I have asked God to give me more understanding. I do know that God is good and the devil is evil. That Jesus came to give us life and life more abundantly and the devil comes to steal, kill and destroy. (John 10:10). The question for me lies in when I perceive something as bad, could it perhaps be God, testing us (not tempting us with evil), refining us and transforming us into His image?

The next day I read the December 18th devotional in the Oswald Chambers book, "My Utmost for His Highest," and got a little confirmation that I was not totally falling off the deep end. Interestingly enough, the scripture that is used is the one that the Holy Spirit whispered to me, when I was on the tarmac with Dustin who had gone into cardiac arrest; after I had lost my son, Forrest, 5 weeks prior; and lastly my mother's death the day before. When I cried out to God at that moment, His answer whispered in my ear was Romans 8:28. I am understanding this a bit more, and never ceased to be amazed at this scripture that God chose that day.

Romans 8:28 *And we know that all things work together for good to them that love God, to them who are the called according to his purpose.*

Chambers quotes, "It is only a faithful person who truly believes that God sovereignly controls his circumstances. We take our circumstances for granted, saying God is in control, but not really believing it. We act as if the things that happen were completely controlled by people (or the devil - my addition). To be faithful in every circumstance means that we have only one loyalty, or object of our faith - the Lord Jesus Christ. God may cause our

circumstances to suddenly fall apart, which may bring the realization of our unfaithfulnness to Him for not recognizing that He had ordained the situation. We never saw what He was trying to accomplish, and that exact event will never be repeated in our life. This is where the test of our faithfulness comes. If we will just learn to worship God even during the difficult circumstances, He will change them for the better very quickly if He so chooses."

"Being faithful to Jesus Christ is the most difficult thing we try to do today. ...The goal of faithfulness is not that we will do work for God, but that He will be free to do His work through us. God calls us to His service and places tremendous responsibilities on us. He expects no complaining on our part and offers no explanation on His part. God wants to use us as He used His own Son."

Faithful in All things...

A Baby... The Baby

Good morning to you all. I pray that the Christmas season has changed you in some positive way, even if it has seemed hard. Families come together and sometimes you wonder if you ever had anything in common. Proverbs reminds us, that no matter what, it is all good, even the sharp edges.

Proverbs 27:17 *Iron sharpeneth iron; so a man sharpeneth the countenance of his friend.*

I want to talk about the song entitled "A Baby Changes Everything." It applies to our lives today.

I am putting the lyrics of the song in quotes followed by my comments.

"Teenage girl, much too young, unprepared for what's to come—a Baby changes everything."

Mary, the mother of Jesus was probably shocked when an Angel of the Lord showed up and said the Holy Ghost was going to overshadow her and conceive the Son of God. This was a change in her life that she was not prepared for. Often, there are changes in our lives that we seem unprepared for, but that God has called us to walk through. Mary accepted the "challenge," and put her full trust in God, when she replied, *"Be it unto me according to thy word."* Can that be our response in life situations?

"Not a ring on her hand. All her dreams and all her plans—a Baby changes everything."

In what seems like confusion and fear in that "it wasn't supposed to happen like this," we can become hopeless and give up. In Mary's time, getting pregnant out of wedlock was one of the worst sins you could do. She was innocent, but people talk. In our own situations, we have our dreams and plans for the future and then a "baby"

Keep Walking...

comes and seems to mess everything all up. People may talk about us and we get hurt and angry and we want to defend ourselves. We have to realize that this is the Lord's battle, not ours and allow Him to have victory in His way (2Chronicles 20:15).

"The man she loves, she's never touched. How will she keep his trust—a Baby changes everything."

When we are earnestly trying our best to follow God, and tough things happen, we tend to go into sin consciousness... meaning we must have broken the law. What did I do wrong?... I should have fasted and prayed longer... I was rude to my neighbor and now I am having to pay.... and on and on. God chose Mary to walk through some tough things in her culture. It wasn't because she had been "bad" but because He knew she would and could do it because she trusted Him. Maybe, just maybe, God has asked you to walk through something that will change the world in some small or large way that we may not understand. I am positive Mary did not understand all this, so we are in good company.

"She has to leave, go far away. Heaven knows she can't stay—a Baby changes everything."

We must know that no matter where we are, that we must accept where we are and move on. Remember, no tent pegs put down in a dangerous place that can destroy us!

"She can feel, it's coming soon. There's no place, there's no room—a Baby changes everything."

All of a sudden, we know everything is getting ready to happen. We may cry out, "Lord, I hear you calling but I don't know what to do, I don't have the skills or the money or the strength to deal with this,

"And she cries! And she cries. Oh, she cries."

We know this part—enough said!

"Shepherds all gather 'round. Up above the star shines down—a Baby changes everything."

Our Shepherd, Jesus, The Shepherd, is there to take care of us and provide everything we need to handle this "Baby" that has been handed to us. Psalm 23 - the Lord is my Shepherd, I shall not want!!!

"Choir of angels sing. Glory to the newborn King—a Baby changes everything."

There's a joy when we look and find Jesus and hear the songs of deliverance being song over us (Psalm 32:7).

"My whole life has turned around. I was lost but now I'm found—a Baby changes everything."

If we, as Mary did, just keep trusting God, even when it seems hopeless, we will come out on the other side, transformed more and more into His image.

Last week we looked at Romans 8:28. I never realized how important verse 29 was to go along with this verse especially when we are talking about tough times.

Romans 8:28 *And we know that all things work together for good to them that love God, to them who are the called according to his purpose. (29) For whom he did foreknow, he also did predestinate to be conformed to the image of his Son, that he might be the firstborn among many brethren.*

The whole reason it all works for good is so that we can be transformed into His image and people can see Him on this earth through us. That is the truest form of evangelism in my opinion. I am becoming convinced that God is not necessarily so interested in all our problems and situations, only our response to them. His greatest plan is to change us - first of all for Him, but for our best good as well.

Keep Walking...

Now—if we can just accept His way and trust that it is the only way, we will probably quit fighting the situation so much and embrace Him. That would be one smiling DAD! A Baby!

The Baby changes everything and boy am I ever grateful!!

(Song - Faith Hill - A Baby Changes Everything - Live on YouTube.)

THE GREAT FARMER

I hope each of you had a wonderful celebration for the birth of Jesus. He should be the "first fruit" of our lives and that is my topic for this week. Sometimes God puts thoughts into my mind about a topic to explore and this week it was "first fruit."

The first fruits are the first ripened part of the harvest that furnish the actual evidence that the entire harvest is on the way. That excites me as a farmer and even more as a Believer.

1 Corinthians 15:20-23 *20But now is Christ risen from the dead, and become the first fruits of them that slept. 21For since by man came death, by man came also the resurrection of the dead. 22For as in Adam all die, even so in Christ shall all be made alive. 23But every man in his own order: Christ the firstfruits; afterward they that are Christ's at his coming.*

Jesus came, lived and died (just like seeds) and then became the one who conquered death. He was the "first fruit," which again is my evidence that the rest of the harvest will come in order (1 Corinthians 15:23).

It explains why there is very little in the New Testament about sorrow, grieving, sadness or death.

I will never forget when I was diving into the Scriptures after losing my boys and mom, trying to figure out how to properly go through their deaths, loss and sadness I was feeling. When I studied the Old Testament, I saw all kinds of legalistic methods of mourning. When I went to the New Testament, I found scriptures that told me to "sorrow not" and asked me why I was sad.

1 Thessalonians 4:13 *But I would not have you to be ignorant, brethren, concerning them which are asleep, that ye sorrow not, even as others which have no hope.*

Keep Walking...

Luke 24:17 *And he said unto them, What manner of communications are these that ye have one to another, as ye walk, and are sad? (They were sad due to the crucifixion of Jesus.)*

The Christmas season could be a difficult time for me. I miss my family and my older son's birthday was Dec. 26th. But if I look to the scriptures I can be encouraged to keep pressing forward.

James 1:18 *Of his own will begat he us with the word of truth, that we should be a kind of firstfruits of his creatures.*

The word "creatures" in the Greek means "original formation or product." God meant for us to live forever, but sin entered in and death came to us in the physical realm. But you know what? God always gets His way. Jesus was the firstfruit and He shows us that we will go the way of God's original plan. Yes we depart from the earth and that was not God's plan, but He redeemed us to live with Him for eternity.

I want to fulfill the plan God has for me on this earth, so I will just have to wait to be part of the bumper crop of Believers that get gathered up with Him. He is one Great Farmer!!

My simple message is "the Baby works!"

Getting Over the I's and My's

Hello to all and peace and grace be with you...cause He is!!

In the Psalm 77 I came across a thought about "I's and "my's" versus "thy's."

Psalm 77:1-9 *¹To the chief Musician, to Jeduthun, A Psalm of Asaph. I cried unto God with my voice, even unto God with my voice; and he gave ear unto me. ²In the day of my trouble I sought the Lord: my sore ran in the night, and ceased not: my soul refused to be comforted. ³I remembered God, and was troubled: I complained, and my spirit was overwhelmed. Selah. ⁴Thou holdest mine eyes waking: I am so troubled that I cannot speak. ⁵I have considered the days of old, the years of ancient times. ⁶I call to remembrance my song in the night: I commune with mine own heart: and my spirit made diligent search. ⁷Will the Lord cast off forever? and will he be favourable no more? ⁸Is his mercy clean gone forever? doth his promise fail for evermore? ⁹Hath God forgotten to be gracious? hath he in anger shut up his tender mercies? Selah.*

In the first verse, we see David crying out to God and God leans in to listen to him. We find in the next eight verses that he is focusing on all that is wrong with him. Basically, he is totally self-occupied. I counted twelve "I's" and "my's" in five verses. In verse three, we see a red flag—he remembered God, and was troubled. The "my's" and "I's" seemed to have a veil over his body, soul and spirit. We see that the final result of any long period of self focus is despondency or being overwhelmed as he says in verse 3. His complaint ends with questioning and misery. That is what happens when we begin to debate the Truth.

Keep Walking...

Fortunately in verses 10 through 12, he ceases his self-occupation and becomes occupied with God.

Psalm 77:10-12 *And I said, This is my infirmity: but I will remember the years of the right hand of the most High. I will remember the works of the LORD: surely I will remember thy wonders of old. I will meditate also of all thy work, and talk of thy doings.*

When we begin to focus on God and all He is, our despondency will vanish. It is the sure cure for misery and despair. He took his "I's" and focused on the "Thy's" and the veil that had blocked him from God was lifted.

And lastly we see what happens when we become occupied with God instead of ourselves:

Psalm 77:13-20 *Thy way, O God, is in the sanctuary: who is so great a God as our God? Thou art the God that doest wonders: thou hast declared thy strength among the people. Thou hast with thine arm redeemed thy people, the sons of Jacob and Joseph. Selah. The waters saw thee, O God, the waters saw thee; they were afraid: the depths also were troubled. The clouds poured out water: the skies sent out a sound: thine arrows also went abroad. The voice of thy thunder was in the heaven: the lightnings lightened the world: the earth trembled and shook. Thy way is in the sea, and thy path in the great waters, and thy footsteps are not known. Thou leddest thy people like a flock by the hand of Moses and Aaron.*

David began to declare and praise God for His greatness and works. So moral of story is take your "I's" and "my's" and all the self-occupation of every detail in life and turn it to a "Thy." You might just see God's clouds pour out the Living water that we needed in the first place!

Keep "Thy-ing!"

SIMPLY ENOUGH

The book of Galatians brings great revelation that Jesus fulfilled the law for us who believe; and that we are no longer condemned in our fleshy living, but convicted. There is such a difference in condemnation and the sweet conviction of the Holy Spirit. Condemnation makes me want to run the other way and give up. It certainly opens the door for self-effort to try to get it "right." Depression and hopelessness jeers at me.

Conviction, on the other hand, reminds me of the sweet presence of the Holy Spirit Who writes on my heart and guides me right back to a deeper, more intimate relationship with God. I'll take conviction any day; that is what freedom from the law does for us.

I want to remind you with a basic statement, "Jesus is simply enough for your every need." Your faith brings to pass what has already been finished. You were already healed, delivered and forgiven, when Jesus died on the cross and clearly told us "it is finished." Quit saying those religious statements like, "I must "die to self." You are already dead to sin if you are in Christ; it just hasn't become a reality to you. We are dead to sin in Christ so we can live a new joyful and grateful life. If we are dead to sin, why do we still sin? It is simply a choice to do so.

Bummer, I wanted to blame it on the devil. As Oswald Chambers so eloquently puts it, "Anything that has even a hint of dejection—spiritually—is always wrong. If I am depressed or burdened, I am to blame, not God or anyone else. Dejection stems from one of two sources - I have either satisfied a lust or I have not had it satisfied. In either case, dejection is the result."

Let's say that I am feeling lonely and my husband is not paying enough attention to me, or that I have been praying for a new car, or a healing or I just went out

Keep Walking...

and spent way too much money. In these examples, I satisfied a lust in shopping or my lust for healing, or a new car or companionship, and even been praying all night long for these and that "lust" has not been satisfied. I can hear those murmuring devils now saying, "but those aren't lusts, those are promises of God" and He is not satisfying those... haha. Good, old Oswald states, "Spiritual lust causes me to demand an answer from God instead of seeking God Himself who gives the answer. The purpose of prayer is to get hold of God, not the answer." Ouch!

The Word and a life of faith (which by the way needs to be exercised like you were preparing for a marathon) is about what has already been accomplished. We need to believe and receive all that because it is already in the store house.

An intimate relationship with God the Father, Jesus and the sweet Holy Spirit is simply enough.

2 Corinthians 11:3 *But I fear, lest by any means, as the serpent beguiled Eve through his subtilty, so your minds should be corrupted from the simplicity that is in Christ.*

Keep walking in the simplicity of the Good News...

Who Do You Go to for Help?

Good evening to you all. I have been preparing a teaching about health and thinking about how careful we must be not to put anything before God. We so often give credit to this product, or this ministry, or this person, or this food that has "healed" us. Isaiah has something very strong to say about that:

Isaiah 30:1-6 *¹Woe to the rebellious children, saith the Lord, that take counsel, but not of me; and that cover with a covering, but not of my spirit, that they may add sin to sin: ²That walk to go down into Egypt, and have not asked at my mouth; to strengthen themselves in the strength of Pharaoh, and to trust in the shadow of Egypt! ³Therefore shall the strength of Pharaoh be your shame, and the trust in the shadow of Egypt your confusion. ⁴For his princes were at Zoan, and his ambassadors came to Hanes. ⁵They were all ashamed of a people that could not profit them, nor be an help nor profit, but a shame, and also a reproach. ⁶The burden of the beasts of the south: into the land of trouble and anguish, from whence come the young and old lion, the viper and fiery flying serpent, they will carry their riches upon the shoulders of young asses, and their treasures upon the bunches of camels, to a people that shall not profit them.*

Here we have the Israelites trusting in the counsel of man, of Egypt, of Pharaoh, (of a doctor, lawyer or Indian Chief), instead of God. They have not asked God for help as you see in verse three, that what they get in return is shame and confusion. In verse six, you see them carrying their riches to Egypt to pay for help instead, of asking God who would give it without price.

How many dollars have we all spent trying to clear up our skin, lose weight, get healed, get happy, get strength, energy, get, get, get, instead of seeking God

Keep Walking...

and His Word for direction? We also get fooled into going to the Christian doctor, the Christian chiropractor or the Christian counselor. Somehow we see or know them as Christian—instead of personally going to God first—we lean on and depend on their "Christian" title and Christianity or faith. We have to be careful in putting the word Christian with a worldly title. Think about it, if they were truly Christian doctors they would pray for you, cast out devils, and lay hands on you; not prescribe a handful of pharmaceuticals and a list of side effects to you. There are doctors who are Christians, but not "Christian doctors." There is a difference.

Now I am certainly not against doctors or medicine. I am against depending on them for every issue I have. Oswald Chambers says, "We show how little love we have for God by preferring to listen to His servants rather than to Him."

In Chapter 31, we see this prophecy continuing:

Isaiah 31:1-3 *[1] Woe to them that go down to Egypt for help; and stay on horses, and trust in chariots, because they are many; and in horsemen, because they are very strong; but they look not unto the Holy One of Israel, neither seek the LORD! [2]Yet he also is wise, and will bring evil, and will not call back his words: but will arise against the house of the evildoers, and against the help of them that work iniquity. [3]Now the Egyptians are men, and not God; and their horses flesh, and not spirit. When the LORD shall stretch out his hand, both he that helpeth shall fall, and he that is holpen shall fall down, and they all shall fail together.*

When we put our trust in men, in flesh, instead of Spirit, it says we shall all fail together. I don't want that for me or them! Lastly we see the King Asa's story. Now before you read this, note that Asa was a great king. He was favored by God because he put all the abominable idols out of all the land, even sacrificing seven hundred oxen and seven thousand sheep and entered into a covenant to seek God with all of his heart and soul (2 Chronicles 15:8-15).

2 Chronicles 16:12-13 *And Asa in the thirty and ninth year of his reign was diseased in his feet, until his disease was exceeding great: yet in his disease he sought not to the LORD, but to the physicians. And Asa slept with his fathers, and died in the one and fortieth year of his reign.*

Again, God was in covenant with Asa, but when he sought man first, God who is jealous for us, turned away from him. We must be ever so mindful to not "think" we are godly people and in the meantime seek after man before God.

Matthew 6:33 *But seek ye first the kingdom of God, and his righteousness; and all these things shall be added unto you.*

God says what He means, and means what He says. Let us be ever mindful of putting Him first in every area of our lives. I promise He will pour out the blessings that will overtake you!

Keep putting Him first!

Muck Boots

Happy "Love" day to you all. I am really not a big Valentine's Day fan, thinking more than it is and probably based on some occultic weird thing like a fat toddler with a bow and arrow that represents love. What I really wish I could do this day is to give you all a hug in real life. What a celebration that would be for me! Since I don't have enough frequent flyer points to fly to each one of you (such as Australia and New Zealand!) I think I will just shovel some stuff that is on my heart to yours!

Now here is a great quote that can certainly preach—"There is no milk without some manure." Some disturbance is the price of growth and accomplishment. "Of course you would know I love this just because it is "farmy." But I think, if we could embrace this "manure", instead of avoiding the piles, we might grow up and mature a little faster.

Scripturally we can look at the book of James' whose theme is "Faith that works."

James 1:2-4 *²My brethren, count it all joy when ye fall into divers temptations; ³Knowing this, that the trying of your faith worketh patience. ⁴But let patience have her perfect work, that ye may be perfect and entire, wanting nothing.*

It has rained four inches in the last few days. Combine that with nine cows, 12 goats 22 chickens and we can talk about some manure. Instead of just parking myself in the comfort of my fire-lit home, I put on my tall rubber boots and go walking through the muck. The key, as always, is "through." It would be stupid to stand in the piles (and piles and piles) of manure. I boldly tromp through and gather eggs, feed animals that will provide meat and milk and come home with the goods. Walking through manure is thus the price of growth and accomplishment.

Keep Walking..

Are you avoiding or denying the manure in your life or are you mucking on through? I promise, although it can be a bit messy, if you truly allow "the trying of your faith" then patience can "have her perfect work, that ye may be perfect and entire wanting nothing." Wow, if walking through manure leaves me wanting nothing, then I'll see ya later. Gotta walk!

I wish I could send you all muck boots to put at your front door as a symbol to "keep walking." Don't be afraid of those piles!! God uses everything to accomplish His best in us. It may take exercising (key word!) faith but remember, faith is knowing that it is already taken care of without seeing it. I promise you when I am out tending the farm in all the muck, I don't look down at those piles but keep moving forward, and of course *"goodness and mercy will follow"* (Psalm 23).

2 Corinthians 5:7 *For we walk by faith, not by sight.* Thank goodness... especially in this message!!

Keep mucking...

A Big Story for His Glory

I pray that you will fully trust God each and every day. We are HIS work and our main job is to know, believe and trust in that. He is working a big story for His glory in us. It promises to be good!

1 Kings 8:56-59 *56 Blessed be the LORD, that hath given rest unto his people Israel, according to all that he promised: there hath not failed one word of all his good promise, which he promised by the hand of Moses his servant. 57 The LORD our God be with us, as he was with our fathers: let him not leave us, nor forsake us: 58 That he may incline our hearts unto him, to walk in all his ways, and to keep his commandments, and his statutes, and his judgments, which he commanded our fathers. 59 And let these my words, wherewith I have made supplication before the LORD, be nigh unto the LORD our God day and night, that he maintain the cause of his servant, and the cause of his people Israel at all times, as the matter shall require:*

If I counted correctly, the above passage has sixteen "He or His" pronouns in it. Verse 56 encourages me in that it says God gives us rest because He *promised* it to us. That one word of His does not fail!

In verse 57, we see that we can cry to God to be consistent and faithful to His promises. We can be reminded that He has been faithful to those in the past and He is the same yesterday, today and forever (**Hebrews 13:8**).

It is always us leaving Him. We are the ones at fault but so often we think He leaves us because we did something wrong. Nope - we are always the ones that move away.

Verse 58 is insistent that this is all about God's work in us. He inclines our hearts unto Him, to walk in His

Keep Walking..

ways, to keep His commandments... this is not about me, but about Him. (May any spiritual self-importance die right here and now).

Lastly He maintains the cause of me—and you—His servants. The word "cause" means verdict. He makes happen all that is supposed to happen—the verdict in us.

As I get older, and hopefully a little wiser, I find great comfort that life is nothing about me. It strips me of ambition in and of myself. That is actually a very difficult place for me because I don't know what to do. I don't want to do anything that is frightening in and of itself.

I pray this new year, that I can ever press into the rest of God doing all the work and accomplishing Himself in me in the earth. With that, I need to be ever sensitive to His voice and I can easily slip into worry about that—that I'll miss hearing Him. But then I am gently nudged back into the above scripture, that if He wants me to hear Him, I will. He will make it happen.

The word says "God in the midst of thee (me)" is mighty. He saves, He rejoices, He rests in His love and joys over me with singing. Forgive me Lord, for thinking I need more.

Zephaniah 3:17 *The LORD thy God in the midst of thee is mighty; he will save, he will rejoice over thee with joy; he will rest in his love, he will joy over thee with singing.*

May each day offer you full assurance of His mighty work in you. It's up to Him! Our story for His glory.

Keep walking...

Do the Dungeon

I hope everyone's new year is going well. If you are in Him and He is in you, no matter what, it is perfect! Just let Him be in everything and I promise it will take the sting out any situation, knowing God is doing a deep and powerful work in this chapter of your life.

I want to share a few recent thoughts from E. Stanley Jones. He calls it "grace in the dungeon." Jones eloquently states if you find grace at all, it must be in the dungeon.

Jeremiah 31:2 *Thus saith the LORD, The people which were left of the sword found grace in the wilderness; even Israel, when I went to cause him to rest.*

Here we find the people to whom his thoughts are addressed. People who were purified in the exile and became the instrument of God through that awful experience of national bondage. The dungeon became a door! You don't have to accept your circumstances as from God, but you can accept them as an opportunity for God to use them to make you creative.

Colossians 4:18 *The salutation by the hand of me Paul. Remember my bonds. Grace be with you. Amen.*

Now we have Paul who is in prison and he tells the church of Colossi that he wants grace to be with them! You would think he would say, "I am in prison—God give me grace." But no, he puts it the other way, "I am in prison and grace be with you." Paul found grace in the dungeon-- enough to spare-- AND pass on to others.

And of course, one of my favorites:

Acts 16:25-26 *And at midnight Paul and Silas prayed, and sang praises unto God: and the prisoners heard them. And suddenly there was a great earthquake, so that the foundations of the prison were shaken: and immediately*

all the doors were opened, and every one's bands were loosed.

God's grace was brought on by the simple acceptance that Paul and Silas were right where God needed them at the time. Instead of whining and complaining they prayed and sang and grace showed up. So much so that all the doors were opened and every one's bands were loosed. That is "grace in the dungeon" with plenty to spare. Even the foundation felt it!!

E. Stanley Jones shares, "A gracious Christian lady said to another: I know you dislike being ill but I find the only thing to do is to get something out of every experience that comes to me. So make your illness give you something."

I absolutely love that. Make your situation give you something that gives God glory. He is in the situation anyway and wants you to find Him!

"Gracious Father, if my circumstances become a dungeon, then help me to find enough grace for myself and plenty to spare for others. Help me not to whine or complain, but to find resources enough to pass on. I know that Your grace is sufficient for me, not merely when life is free and open, but when life turns into a dungeon. You promise me your grace in my time of need. I want to be a good steward of it and share it with all those around me."

Do the dungeon.

Keep walking...

Don't Despise the Valleys

Good morning to each one of you. Recently I was around a group of women who were sharing how much they were being attacked by the enemy in their homes, marriages, children, etc. One shared that she was trying to figure out what she was doing wrong. We should not be surprised by the "attacks." That is simply Satan doing his job and he is good at it. Are we good at being disciples of Christ (our job) in the midst of this war for our lives and those all around us?

We call ourselves disciples. A disciple is a "learner" according to the Greek language. We learn by following someone and listening, observing and taking some mental notes. Baby ducks follow mom all around the barnyard and water learning how to maneuver in life for the best outcome. Perhaps the ducklings are taking baby duck-mental notes for future use. If the mother encounters danger, her actions teach the babies what the best way to move through it might be.

As disciples of Christ, we must follow Him by observing His life on earth through the Word. We too, have to follow Him through some of the worst situations all the way to death and out the other side to resurrection! Baby ducks don't decide to "sit this one out" when an attack comes. They must learn and grow through it. We must not expect to do that either. In other words, don't passively sit out the attack. Make the situation give you something that you would never have gotten if you hadn't gone through it. Something from the throne room of God Himself. He is present in every situation, even the evil. He says He will never leave us or forsake us, so He is there.

Expect His grace in your time of need; don't expect failure or fear failure. Jesus cared little about success or failure. The story of Jesus is a story of an apparent failure—rejected by His own nation and then cruci-

Keep Walking..

fied, ending up on a cross. A faith that has a cross (an instrument of death) at its center cannot be a faith that worships success and expects perfect families, perfect marriages, perfect finances, and perfect health.

I do not have to succeed; I only have to be true to God. Success and failure are in His hands. Don't be in bondage to success in every area of your life. Our call is to trust and obey God in all things. If the following of Christ takes some really tough paths, remember it is His job to get you to your mountain top. I heard this statement recently, "You will die if you stay on the mountain top. There is not water or food on the top. We must go to the valleys of life for water and nourishment to make it to the next mountaintop. Don't despise the valleys. They are necessary for the very life that we live."

Remember Job who went through a horrendous time. God Himself said Job was a righteous and upright man, thus he really wasn't a "sinner" who needed to repent. But when Job was in the very presence of the Living God, you can imagine the humility needed. Basically he repented for his attitude during his suffering. Wow -that really can penetrate many of our lives at the core. We suffer, we beg God to get us out of it, we demand that He answer our prayers and hurry up, or we simply give up in believing this has anything to do with His will for our lives. Certainly we say, this tough time is not from God. Maybe, just maybe, it is. The key is to expect exceeding joy. It is a promise of God, no matter how the valley seems.

My favorite scripture, when we cry out to God to ask "why" is **1 Peter 4:12-13:** *Beloved, think it not strange concerning the fiery trial which is to try you, as though some strange thing happened unto you: But rejoice, inasmuch as ye are partakers of Christ's sufferings; that, when his glory shall be revealed, ye may be glad also with exceeding joy.*

Keep walking towards your exceeding joy...

Keep Walking...

CAN YOU RECEIVE?

Many of us find it easy to give and help others but when help is offered to us we politely decline. We don't receive their gift towards us. Maybe we don't feel like we deserve it, maybe we don't want people to think we don't have all of our ducks in a row, or maybe we just want to appear perfect and do it all ourselves. We are bad receivers and we tend to be even worse in the Christian aspect.

In looking at the Beatitudes, we see Jesus beginning to teach. It is the study of "the happy ones."

Matthew 5:3 *Blessed are the poor in spirit: for theirs is the kingdom of heaven.*

Matthew 5:4 *Blessed are they that mourn: for they shall be comforted.*

Matthew 5:5 *Blessed are the meek: for they shall inherit the earth.*

If you look at the first three beatitudes, they are all "receptive" instead of assertive. They are written as all passive virtues. First we see the poor in spirit given the kingdom of heaven. They don't belong to heaven, heaven belongs to them! If you take a minute and think about that, it means that all the powers and resources in heaven are at their disposal. They are backed by the universe.

The second beatitude is specific. It says if you mourn, the reward is comfort. If you dissect this word, you find that "com" means together and "fortis" means brave. We are brave together - that would be you, me, God, Christ and the Holy Spirit. What a team to be on, and certainly far greater than depression.

Lastly, the meek inherit the earth. We saw in verse three that you inherit heaven, now you get the earth. "Meek" is probably one of my favorite words. It is not

Keep Walking..

a wimp or a weakness, but a controlled strength. That would be our Jesus! All the power on heaven and earth at his Word and yet His demeanor of gentleness and kindness could fool you into thinking He doesn't have much to offer. That is why you need to base your faith in the Word and not some picture of a long-haired and thin man from Sunday School.

All of these beatitudes are pretty awesome. We are given heaven, earth and comfort.

The requirements:

- IF we don't think too highly of ourselves and our own self-efforts,
- IF we take our losses to Jesus and He exchanges them for comfort,
- IF we would walk with all of heaven and earth on the inside of us, but never flaunting it to gain attention for ourselves.

All of this requires receiving. Can you receive the power of these first few Beatitudes? Or do you cower down in your past or present sins listening to how unworthy you are of anything? If you listen to that "other voice" I would question your true salvation. If you are truly a child of God, you are forgiven and every gift is from God. We don't earn gifts, they must be received. You are an heir, and heirs always receive!!

Keep receiving...

Keep Walking...

No Mixture

Our topic today is a discussion on the Law versus Grace. The scriptures have shown us that when you try to mix both plans in your life it isn't going to work. It's kind of like buying a new house but still trying to live in the old one. You never get grounded with roots, but are just tossed back and forth between houses. Neither house gets utilized or launched into its fullness. Rick always says that this is why God closed the Red Sea. The Israelites would probably have gotten a little freaked out and run back the other way. God wanted them fully present and focused on the opportunities of the new Promised Land.

Hebrews 10:9b reminds us that ..".*He taketh away the first, that He may establish the second,"* meaning that the law had to be abolished so the New Covenant could come, more specifically so that Jesus could come!

I was reading in Psalms this morning and came across this scripture:

Psalm 62:9 *Surely men of low degree are vanity, and men of high degree are a lie: to be laid in the balance, they are altogether lighter than vanity.*

I love the notes from the Dake's Bible on this passage. He says, "Don't trust in people of low degree, for they cannot help. They may be willing, but they have no ability to help. Don't trust in people of high degree—the ungodly rich—for they promise much but perform nothing. They cause you to hope, but mock at your expectation. Hence, both those who are common and the ungodly rich are lighter than vanity, for they disappoint people who put their trust in them."

Every time I read this scripture, it makes me think of how life without Jesus is vanity. If I take all my good points, my university degrees, my finances, my talents, etc., and weigh them all together I may have a few good days. Without Jesus, these will perhaps suffice until I take my last breath. After that, hell is not interested in my nutrition degrees, my proficiency as a gardener or my ability to take care of myself. All of that is useless, meaningless and hopeless without Jesus.

I promised myself I would keep this short but I have a bit more to add. This scripture was brought up on last week's call:

2 Corinthians 3:14 *But their minds were blinded: for until this day remaineth the same vail untaken away in the reading of the old testament; which vail is done away in Christ.*

When we try to stay in the Old Testament/Law, then perhaps the veil is still in place and we can't get the fullness of Jesus. It goes back to the beginning of this newsletter. You can't mix the old with the new. It becomes a hazy mess.

Matthew 9:17 *Neither do men put new wine into old bottles: else the bottles break, and the wine runneth out, and the bottles perish: but they put new wine into new bottles, and both are preserved.*

Let the Old Testament show you Jesus. There are many types, shadows and prophecies. When we look for Jesus, we will find Him. We can read the Old Testament with great hope and can see that, all along, God had a perfect plan. His name was Jesus. Out with the old, in with the new might just be that New Year's message! More importantly and realistically, learn from the old year (Old Covenant) and focus on the "new" plan God has for you which is more grace and more freedom!

Keep focusing on the new and learning from the old...

Using Everything

I have started a new, actually very old, devotion book called "Abundant Living," by E. Stanley Jones. (The copyright is MCMXLII (1942) and the person who gave this book to someone, signed it September 5, 1946.) It discusses a topic we think as "new" and that is the connection between body, soul and spirit. The preface talks about different doctors and their estimate of the percentage of people who pass on mental and spiritual sickness to their physical bodies. Their estimates ranged from 40-85%.

I found it very interesting that the American Medical Association officially approved the statement of a physician in 1931, that the percentage is about 50. You sure wouldn't know that the AMA had anything to do with spiritual and mental aspects of healing disease today.

I consider the following to be a very balanced statement made by E. Stanley Jones on healing :

"We believe that God heals the body in one or more of these ways:

1. By medicine
2. By surgery
3. By scientific nutrition
4. By climate
5. By mental suggestion
6. By deliverance from underlying fears, resentments, self-centeredness and guilt
7. By the direct action of the Spirit of God upon our bodies
8. By the resurrection.

Some ailments may have to wait for that final curing, the resurrection, for we live in a mortal world where the body is bound to break down sometime. In that case we can not merely bear the infirmity, we can use it. We can take it up into the purpose of our lives and transmute it into character and achievement. God will cure you through one or more of the first seven ways; or if not, He will give you the power to use, and to make it contribute until the final cure in the resurrection."

So often we feel guilty or think we have a lack of faith if we have to take medicine, or even a vitamin. If you feel guilty, you have probably moved back under the law, as the purpose of the law was to condemn.

Ephesians 2:8-9 *For by grace are ye saved through faith; and that not of yourselves: it is the gift of God: Not of works, lest any man should boast.*

Spiritual things can be "works" if we decide to do them ourselves versus being prompted to do them by the Spirit of God. This year, may we all be led by the Holy Spirit in all that we do, that God may get the glory. If we are doing things based on a law we have created for ourselves, versus doing as the Holy Spirit leads (and sometimes that may be a unusual surprise!), we only receive the outcome or rewards from our own accomplishments.

Matthew 6:1 *Take heed that ye do not your alms before men, to be seen of them: otherwise ye have no reward of your Father which is in heaven.*

Matthew 6:4 *That thine alms may be in secret: and thy Father which seeth in secret himself shall reward thee openly.*

We can either receive the rewards from our own work or someone else, or we can receive the rewards from God. I promise God's are greater than man's! Let the Spirit of God lead you this year. You will go through some nice terrain and probably a few deserts, swamps and high mountains. Regardless, He will be with you through it all and be creating some mighty "footage" for others if you will allow it. If you pursue Him, there will always

Keep Walking...

be peace, even though it may seem like an unusual direction.

2 Corinthians 1:3-4 *Blessed be God, even the Father of our Lord Jesus Christ, the Father of mercies, and the God of all comfort; Who comforteth us in all our tribulation, that we may be able to comfort them which are in any trouble, by the comfort wherewith we ourselves are comforted of God.*

It's all good if you are in Christ! Don't despise anything you go through—it's all usable!!

Keep walking...

AFFLICTION WORKS

We have talked a lot about "work" in the kingdom of God. We know that works can't save us, don't make us more righteous, and don't earn us spiritual pats on the back. In fact when you have religious works going on, unless it's led by God for His glory, then you are only getting tired, frustrated and wishing Jesus would hurry up and come. Yes we do know that faith without works is dead, so the question is how do we practice "works" in the gospel of grace and of what benefit do works bring to our daily life in Christ?

James 2:20 *But wilt thou know, O vain man, that faith without works is dead?*

The above scripture tells me that I must show my faith and God given gifts in how I live. I am not sure where that became working in the nursery every week, cooking meals for the homeless, being in the choir, etc. However, all those things are wonderful if we are called to do them and anointed to "show our faith" in doing them.

I see the scripture as saying, that if God has given you a gift then you need to share it with others so they can get the benefit of seeing Him in you. If I knew how to speak fluent Russian and never spoke it when around people who needed language interpretation, then my gift would be wasted. In other words, "knowing the Russian language", without using it to help others, is dead."

On another note, what benefit does work bring to us in our daily Christian walk? Two scriptures jumped out at me as I thought about this:

2 Corinthians 4:12 *So then death worketh in us, but life in you.*

2 Corinthians 4:17-18 *For our light affliction, which is but for a moment, worketh for us a far more exceeding*

Keep Walking...

and eternal weight of glory; While we look not at the things which are seen, but at the things which are not seen: for the things which are seen are temporal; but the things which are not seen are eternal.

The Greek word for "worketh" in verse 12 is "to be active, efficient, effectual and to be mighty in." So we see that a benefit of works in us is death, but life for others. Now that sounds a little intense but if you think about it, anytime we allow sin or temptation to "die" in us, it is a testimony of what God has done in our lives, therefore, benefitting others. This death should be working in us every day of our lives so we can become more like Him.

The greatest example of this "deaths works" is the death of Jesus Himself. He took on ALL sin and entered death as the greatest testimony and life for all of mankind.

In verse 17, we see that our light affliction works for us. The word "worketh" in this passage means to "work fully, to accomplish, and by implication to finish." Thus our afflictions (Greek - pressure, anguish, tribulation) are a way that God sovereignly allows trial, tribulations and even demonic influences to fully accomplish His greatest plan in our life so we can finish this race successfully.

In summary, death and afflictions "work" for us. If that is what the Word says, why do we hate going through them so much? My best answer is that we try to do it in our own flesh and it hurts waaaaaaaaaay too bad. The only way to go through these things successfully is hand in hand with Jesus. Then, and only then, does the beautiful vessel get formed.

I don't make pottery, but we all know that if the pot has a lump or flaw, it gets beat on and thrown back on the wheel. Let God "beat" on you with His loving hands so that you can become His greatest vessel.

Keep Walking..

Then, and only then, can He pour Himself through you fully. Otherwise you leak and make a mess!!

Don't despise or fear the potter's wheel.

Keep trusting the Potter.

Keep Walking...

The Story for Grief

I have gotten so much out of 2 Corinthians lately that I thought that I would share some of it with you. My theme always seems to be grief, suffering and loss, but hopefully with the application of the Word we can see that, with God, it is simply a journey of love.

Last night I heard a wonderful teaching on how the best book in dealing with grief is the Bible. Of course, we know that, but the speaker said that the Bible is the "life-death-life" story and is the best story to find our hope. He went on to say that we live in the middle of this story and thus we have suffering.

We can look at upright, God-fearing men in Job and Paul and find that God's chosen did not escape suffering. Instead, He chose them to go through dark places. Yes, Jesus cares about a person's suffering but he cares so much more about the person. Wow, chosen by God. He certainly sees something I can't see in myself and that is how I can bow before the "mystery."

It seems as having a hope in God is somewhat of being a rebel against the world. Hope doesn't come naturally, it takes a decision. Death is not the final word. We can have hope because, ultimately, death dies. Thus, having hope in God, is being a rebel against the worldly ways of grief and suffering. Rebel, I shall be!!

1 Corinthians 15:26 *The last enemy that shall be destroyed is death.*

In 2nd Corinthians chapter six, Paul is talking about being a minister of God and begins to list a whole barrage of things (grief), that come with that in verses 4-10.

2 Corinthians 6:4-10 *But in all things approving ourselves as the ministers of God, in much patience, in afflictions, in necessities, in distresses, In stripes, in*

imprisonments, in tumults, in labours, in watchings, in fastings; By pureness, by knowledge, by longsuffering, by kindness, by the Holy Ghost, by love unfeigned, By the word of truth, by the power of God, by the armour of righteousness on the right hand and on the left, By honour and dishonour, by evil report and good report: as deceivers, and yet true; As unknown, and yet well known; as dying, and, behold, we live; as chastened, and not killed; As sorrowful, yet alway rejoicing; as poor, yet making many rich; as having nothing, and yet possessing all things.

In verses nine and ten, it seems like he says something, only to contradict it in the next words.

2 Corinthians 6:9-10 *As unknown, and yet well known; as dying, and, behold, we live; as chastened, and not killed; As sorrowful, yet always rejoicing; as poor, yet making many rich; as having nothing, and yet possessing all things.*

Paul was comparing himself to the standards of the world. If you look at it from God's point of view (which outranks the world's) you are well known, living, always rejoicing, making others rich and possessing all things!!

Let me give you two other versions of this scripture. The first is from the Amplified Bible which fleshes out the KJV into a little more Greek. The second is from the New Testament in Modern English which I found in my mom's stuff when she changed her address—now lives with God.

2 Corinthians 6:9-10 (Amp): *(We are treated) as unknown and ignored (by the world), and (yet we are) well-known and recognized (by God and His people); as dying and yet here we are alive; as chastened by suffering and (yet) not killed; As grieved and mourning, yet (we are) always rejoicing; as poor (ourselves ,yet) bestowing riches on many; as having nothing , and (yet in reality) possessing all things.*

Keep Walking...

2 Corinthians 6:9-10 (Modern English) *Called "imposters" we must be true, called "nobodies" we must be in the public eye. Never far from death, yet here we are still alive, always "going through it" yet never "going under." We know sorrow, yet our joy is inextinguishable. We have "nothing to bless ourselves with," yet we bless others with true riches. We are penniless and yet in reality we have everything worth having.*

My point today is simply to stick with God. He has a perfect way. Be chosen of God and go willingly with Him through whatever He has called you to walk through. Walking in that identity will defeat whatever the Devil tries to hand you!

Keep walking...

KNOW AND CALL

I was interested in the heading of Psalm 18 that I was reading the other day. Its title is the "First Psalm of Deliverance."

Psalm 18:2-3 *The LORD is my rock, and my fortress, and my deliverer; my God, my strength, in whom I will trust; my buckler, and the horn of my salvation, and my high tower. I will call upon the LORD, who is worthy to be praised: so shall I be saved from mine enemies.*

There is no method in this "deliverance." Instead it is simply a declaration of who King David knows God to be. He is resting in the Lord. He knows exactly who God is, what His heart stands for, and the power of the Great I AM. He is saying that he has a need and God is his Rock, his Fortress, his Deliverer, his Strength, his Buckler, and his High Tower. That sounds like pure safety and protection from ANYTHING! David's and our job is simply to know and call. Really? Could it be that easy; just to know and call?

Psalm 18:28 *For thou wilt light my candle: the LORD my God will enlighten my darkness.*

Just know and call on the Lord and He will bring you out of trouble and darkness. The word "wilt" is present tense. You might be saying, "Yes, that's my God, but I really need to pray an hour a day, repent and ask for forgiveness, and then get someone to pray a deliverance prayer over me." That is all fine, but you don't have to if you really know and have a relationship with Jesus. Your deliverance could go something like this:

"Lord, the Holy Spirit has brought to my attention that I have uttered some slander (fill in the blank) against people at work. Thank you so much that You love me enough to show me this so I can "know and call" on You.

Keep Walking...

Your love for me is so great that I have already been forgiven some 2000 years ago for this sin. I acknowledge Your love for me and Your patience in growing me up to be more like You. Thank You so much for being my Savior, for convicting me of sin, so I can just praise who You are in my life. I am not worthy, but you make me worthy in Your eyes. I so appreciate Your willingness to sanctify me so I can become more like You. You are worthy to be praised!!"

1 Corinthians 1:30 *But of him are ye in Christ Jesus, who of God is made unto us wisdom, and righteousness, and sanctification, and redemption:*

He's the One that has been made unto us wisdom and righteousness. Who sanctified and redeems us. We just have to be "in Christ" and "know and call!" His answer is on the inside of us. Wow, He is that close!!

Keep knowing and calling...

Accomplishing Talent

I pray that this message will speak to any "stuckness" you may have in doing all that God wants to do through you!

Matthew 25:15 *And unto one he gave five talents, to another two, and to another one; to every man according to his several ability; and straightway took his journey.*

Matthew 25:18 *But he that had received one went and digged in the earth, and hid his lord's money.*

Matthew 25:25 *And I was afraid, and went and hid thy talent in the earth: lo, there thou hast that is thine.*

Almost the whole chapter contains Jesus' words written in red. That alone should grab our attention! In verse 15, the lord is handing out talents. If we look at this closely, we see that he gave talents "according to his several ability, "meaning that each man had the skills and abilities to produce different amounts of fruit.

Let's look at some Greek words that blew me away. The word "several" means pertaining to self, and the word "ability" means a force, a miraculous power. What Jesus is trying to get across is that HE knew what HE had put on the inside of each of these three people to accomplish, and they, by faith, had to trust that or not. We see that the first two guys believed in God and what He could accomplish in them. The third guy didn't trust what God had given him. He was afraid and buried his talent in the earth. How often does God give us "ability" or miraculous power that we bury, because in our human strength we don't think we can do it—so we just don't?

Matthew 25:23 *His lord said unto him, Well done, good and faithful servant; thou hast been faithful over a few things, I will make thee ruler over many things: enter thou into the joy of thy lord.*

Keep Walking...

Here we see what happens if we trust God's ability in us. A faithful servant - faithful in that we don't know how we can do something, but know the One who does, who lives in us. When we trust Him, He will raise us up and help us walk on this crazy planet called earth, manifesting a countenance of joy.

What miraculous power has God put in you, that maybe by fear, you have buried? A faithful servant is one that doesn't know how, but knows the One who does!

Don't bury your talent...

THE NEARNESS OF GOD

A few months ago our conference call focused on Col. 1:27 which says "Christ in us, the hope of glory." God is not "out there, or up there, or over there," but right there in you!! We are not trying to get Him to heal you, or deliver you or provide for you or give you peace. He already accomplished all of that more than 2000 years ago on the cross. In other words, we don't have to beg and plead for Him to move on our behalf, He simply already has!!

I was reading a scripture this morning that so spoke to me on that topic- the nearness of God's Word.

Deuteronomy 30:11-14 *For this commandment which I command thee this day, it is not hidden from thee, neither is it far off. It is not in heaven, that thou shouldest say, Who shall go up for us to heaven, and bring it unto us, that we may hear it, and do it? Neither is it beyond the sea, that thou shouldest say, Who shall go over the sea for us, and bring it unto us, that we may hear it, and do it? But the word is very nigh unto thee, in thy mouth, and in thy heart, that thou mayest do it.*

God's Word is not hidden from you, nor far off in heaven, nor beyond the seas, but it is near you and in your mouth and heart. The last few words say *"thou mayest do it."* I love how the amplified version says it. It says, "you can do it."

We can do this thing people, God has made sure of that in every way. He has given us the commandment of love and His Living Word, along with the Holy Spirit to help teach us. God's Word is plainly revealed and recorded in the most simple language that nobody can rightfully claim that it is hard to understand because of its hidden meaning. (Dakes Bible notes). I pondered that thought because often it seems so hard to understand. I wonder

Keep Walking...

if it is because we wrestle with the truth of the scriptures with our fleshly minds. We can't believe it could be total truth because we try to apply our worldly knowledge and our physical senses to something that has to be believed and received by faith which is a spiritual endeavor.

The Living Word—the power of God—is in our mouth and our heart. That means we need to speak it. If our mind is drawing us into temptation or dark places that are not of God, we need to think and speak God's promises. If we do that often enough, our minds will get renewed, our heart's changed, and our mouth will speak the abundance of the heart!

Luke 6:45 *A good man out of the good treasure of his heart bringeth forth that which is good; and an evil man out of the evil treasure of his heart bringeth forth that which is evil: for of the abundance of the heart his mouth speaketh.*

What you are desiring in your heart and your words is not up there or out there but in there... that close! Appropriate God's nearness in every area of your life.

Be right there...

The Sound of Many Waters

There are over 683 uses of the word water or waters in the Bible. I probably could do books on water for the rest of my life and still not cover the topic. If you know me, I am all about water. If you ever see me, I usually always have a bottle of water in my hand. To me it is life, and it literally is in so many ways!

The most important thing about water is that it is a major constituent of life and is vital. That is true of the two atoms of hydrogen and one atom of oxygen that form water and about the Living Word. I think it is interesting that God would use water in so many ways to discuss the triuneness of who He is; to a molecule containing three atoms. No matter what we do, through pollution, technology or any other scheme, the amount of water on the earth today is the same as since creation. Just like our God, He is the same today, yesterday and forever.

Hebrews 13:8 *Jesus Christ the same yesterday, and to day, and for ever.*

Water covers 71% of the earth's surfaces and our bodies are approximately 70% water. The blood that pulses through our veins that gives us life is 90% water. This is a lot of water and we can see how important it is to God as He created us this way.

Revelation 1:15 *And his feet like unto fine brass, as if they burned in a furnace; and his voice as the sound of many waters.*

Ezekiel 43:2 *And, behold, the glory of the God of Israel came from the way of the east: and his voice was like a noise of many waters: and the earth shined with his glory.*

Now we see that when God speaks to us, His voice, the Words He speaks, sounds like a lot of rushing wa-

Keep Walking...

ter. That is so significant to me. He created us and our environment "watery", and then speaks the Living Water to our dry and thirsty lives. He invites us to know the Father, The Son and The Holy Spirit in a deep and mighty way, the three "atoms" if you will of the most abundant thing on earth that is vital to life.

In summary, we see that water is made of three atoms and is one of the most powerful substances on earth. Even after our abuse of water, we still have the same amount, some of it is just more polluted. Regardless, it is still there. Finally we see that Jesus Christ is the same "amount" as ever and His voice gushes out life for all to hear.

He even deals with our pollution!!

I pray that you will hear the voice of the Lord... "the sound of many waters."

Jump in the river...

Water and Fire

Good morning, I hope you are thirsty as the water topic continues!! Last week we saw that the voice of the Lord is like the sound of many waters; and in the natural creation it is a major constituent of living things and is vital to life. We can't live without it. Now that is TRUTH!!

I want to share a few more interesting facts about water. First of all, it is a universal solvent. I looked up the word solvent to make sure I had it right in my head and yes, its meaning is that it has the power to dissolve everything. However, God really did use all of His creation as a parable for us to see His greatness, as the word solvent also means that you are able to pay all debts!! God can dissolve anything because the debts, the dirt, the irritants of life have been paid!!

1 John 1:9 *If we confess our sins, he is faithful and just to forgive us our sins, and to cleanse us from all unrighteousness.*

The word "cleanse" in the Greek means to make pure. Purity is a word I was not really familiar with in my younger, wilder days. What a blessing to find out that I could be washed clean and start over. I remember feeling like a virgin bride when I married Rick, because of this scripture. What a godly delight to start a marriage in this way, just like God intended. By His grace He allowed it even when I had botched up my past. Ahhhh, clean as clean can be because of His "water."

Isaiah 58:11 *And the LORD shall guide thee continually, and satisfy thy soul in drought, and make fat thy bones: and thou shalt be like a watered garden, and like a spring of water, whose waters fail not.*

His spring never runs dry and never fails!

Keep Walking...

The second fact that we all know about water is that it puts out fire. Fiery trials, hell fire and even refining fire need to be put out in God's perfect timing. His Word does this mightily if we "jump in the river!"

Psalm 66:12 *Thou hast caused men to ride over our heads; we went through fire and through water: but thou broughtest us out into a wealthy place.*

God's elements are perfect. We go through the fire, He waters it and brings us out to a wealthy place. I am so grateful to be in Him and Him in me. Quite refreshing, I might add!

Psalm 42:7 *Deep calleth unto deep at the noise of thy waterspouts: all thy waves and thy billows are gone over me.*

(Song.- "Deep Calls to Deep" by David and Nicole Binion on YouTube)

Stay wet!

He in Me and I in Him

I hope (confident expectation) that you are having a blessed spring day. We are blessed, because He is blessed, and we are in Him. I am reminded of an example that helped me to really get this. If I place a piece of paper in a book, then the paper will experience everything the book experiences. If I throw it in the water, the paper goes with it. If I burn it, it gets burned. If I handle the book, it gets handled, and so on. So if Christ is in me and I in Him, then I can experience everything He experiences and vice versa.

Many of you know that I am back in school taking some core classes to enter the nursing program. School is very different than when I was last there in 1985. Computers were barely out and I remember paying someone $1 per page to type my thesis. Now everything is by computer! The learning curve has been steep, but praise God, I am stimulating those new neuron pathways!! While school and new skills are frustrating, I continue to lean into the Word. I feel like God has always meant for me to be in the medical field, but the eating disorder demon won out and I ended up studying nutrition to build up a fortress of knowledge and defense to protect myself. At 56 years of age, I decided to follow God in this area. So, if it is true that He has called me to move forward, then I must expect Him to get me through computers and all the other new skills that will stretch my aging brain.

2 Corinthians 1:21 *Now he which stablisheth us with you in Christ, and hath anointed us, is God;*

1 John 2:27 *But the anointing which ye have received of him abideth in you, and ye need not that any man teach you: but as the same anointing teacheth you of all things, and is truth, and is no lie, and even as it hath taught you, ye shall abide in him.*

Keep Walking...

What an awesome encouragement. I don't have to try to "be anointed" but the anointing is Him and "it" lives in me and teaches me!!

Exodus 31:3-5 *And I have filled him with the spirit of God, in wisdom, and in understanding, and in knowledge, and in all manner of workmanship, to devise cunning works, to work in gold, and in silver, and in brass, And in cutting of stones, to set them, and in carving of timber, to work in all manner of workmanship.*

This has always been a favorite scripture of mine. Somewhere, somehow, talents and gifts and knowledge to accomplish things had to start. There had to be a beginning. God did not build metal working, gemology or construction schools first and then proceed to teach people. No, He by the Spirit of God filled them in wisdom, understanding and in ALL manner of workmanship. With that in mind, and since He is the same today, yesterday and forever, I am counting on Him to get me through school. That is a restful place to be and puts me in that place of trusting Him once more.

Psalm 23:2-3 *"He makes me lie down in green pastures; He leads me beside still waters; He restores my soul; He leads me in the paths of righteousness for His names sake."* He, He, He NOT me, me, me.

If God has called you to do something, trust Him as the anointing that will teach you and make it happen.

Walking in Him, walking in the anointing.

Keep Walking..

God is Hands On

Oh happy day to you all! Do you ever feel like you are not sure you are going to make it, or if life is always going to be the same, no matter how hard you try, or even, don't try?

Psalm 138:8 *The LORD will perfect that which concerneth me: thy mercy, O LORD, endureth for ever: forsake not the works of thine own hands.*

I came across this scripture today and once again, the pressure is off of me to worry about this. Let me define a few words in the Hebrew language and then put it into, as my pastor often says, "Good, old Georgia redneck words."

The word "perfect" means to end, finish, accomplish, to come to an end. The word "concerneth" means to be up to, or over against. The word "forsake" means to slacken. And lastly the word "hands" in this scripture signifies an open hand meaning power and direction. It is the Lord, (not me) that accomplishes and brings to an end those things that I am over against. He is not going to be slack about His work in my life but will accomplish it in His power and direction.

Philippians 1:6 *Being confident of this very thing, that he which hath begun a good work in you will perform it until the day of Jesus Christ.*

The simple emphasis is that it is US that needs to be confident that it is God that is doing the work and will continue until Jesus comes back. Phew, I'm safe!

1 Peter 5:10 *But the God of all grace, who hath called us unto his eternal glory by Christ Jesus, after that ye have suffered a while, make you perfect, stablish, strengthen, settle you.*

Maybe you have suffered a bit in your walk in life, but don't despair, the God of ALL grace is making you perfect which means in Greek, "repaired." God is really fixing us up!!!

Keep confident...

Keep Walking...

Freedom Not Fear

I remember when Dustin was in the Tampa Veterans Hospital and a sign outside said something to the effect of "the price of freedom is inside." Freedom costs something. It costs the lives of our brave men and women who have fought in the military. We can get "free" food stamps, "free" medical care and even "free" money in a sense. But somebody is paying... and paying... and paying for this free stuff. It never ends, someone has to keep paying. So yes, free stuff is an option and you can only hope that it will last long enough to get you through. Underneath, there is always a fear that is might not. That is a human anxiety that erodes the very fabric of our lives, keeps us self-focused, and always in a self-preservation mode. With that life, we are usually unable to fully serve others. True freedom is our other choice. True freedom costs the ultimate sacrifice of Christ.

John 8:32 *And ye shall know the truth, and the truth shall make you free.*

John 8:36 *If the Son therefore shall make you free, ye shall be free indeed.*

The word free in the Greek means to liberate or deliver. If I am bound to the "free stuff" then I am not delivered but dependent on it. If "it" goes, I go. When our freedom comes from our relationship with Jesus, then we are liberated, (which means to be set free from slavery!). We never have to hope that "someone" is going to continue to pay for the "free stuff," because in Christ, the price was paid once and for all.

1 Corinthians 7:23 *Ye are bought with a price; be not ye the servants of men.*

Our freedom has been bought with a price. If we choose "free stuff" we are the servants of men. The following scripture indicates that whatever you serve should be able to take care of you.

Jeremiah 2:28 *But where are thy gods that thou hast made thee? let them arise, if they can save thee in the time of thy trouble: for according to the number of thy cities are thy gods, O Judah.*

We choose "free stuff" because we fear that we can't take care of ourselves... it just seems easier. Easier costs. It costs our freedom and shalom peace of mind, body and spirit.

1 John 4:18 *There is no fear in love; but perfect love casteth out fear: because fear hath torment. He that feareth is not made perfect in love.*

After spending several years in ministry and trying to cast out spirits of fear, I have come to the conclusion that Jesus never did. He cast out unclean spirits, dumb spirits and spirits of infirmity and a few others, but I haven't seen where He cast out spirits of fear. I do see that if you don't want fear in your life, the answer is accepting the Perfect Presence of Perfect Love of Christ in you. In the presence of God, there is no fear. If you have fear in your life, may I suggest that you acknowledge, believe and walk in the power of Perfect Love in you? If I am in fear, the scripture says that my relationship with Christ is lacking.

Instead of going to another ministry, reading another book or, or, or... why not just believe the Living Word? You might just find true freedom! Jesus didn't cast out fear because it was about a deep, believing and passionate relationship with Perfect Love. The Word says in **2 Timothy 1:7** that, *"God has not given us a spirit of fear, but of power, love and a sound mind."* It takes the power of God, love and a sound mind to have relationship.

May I suggest that instead of trying to "get" freedom that you head on over to the layaway window and pick up your gift of freedom. Gifts are free, you don't work for them—just receive!

Be free and receive everyday!

Keep Walking...

God's not Mad

I pray that you have a huge respect for the freedom we have in this country and in our Saviour! Please remember our active duty soldiers, our wounded warriors and our veterans.

Our topic today is about sin. So many religions and denominations want to scare you, condemn you and remind you that if you don't get your act straight that you are going straight to hell because God is mad! They go on to say that if there is anything wrong in your life, there is probably disobedience or rebellion that you need to figure out and repent for and get right. It seems to me that this is false theology looking at the following scriptures:

2 Corinthians 7:10 *For godly sorrow worketh repentance to salvation not to be repented of: but the sorrow of the world worketh death.*

Using some of the Greek definitions of the words, "worketh" and "repentance," this verse goes something like this: *When the Holy Spirit does His job (and not us trying to figure it all out!), He will convict us of our sin and because we love God, our sorrow of recognizing how we have been deceived "worketh" or fully accomplishes repentance.* This word repentance means a reversal of another decision. If we are just bummed out because we didn't get our way and got caught, then this type of sorrow "fully accomplishes" death.

We see an example of this in the following verse:

2 Samuel 12:13 *And David said unto Nathan, I have sinned against the LORD. And Nathan said unto David, The LORD also hath put away thy sin; thou shalt not die.*

This was a true conviction by David and the LORD put his sin away. The Holy Spirit NEVER comes to condemn us or box us into a corner, but comes to convict us. When we trust the full crucifixion and resurrection message, that we are forgiven of all past, present and future sins, then we don't have to beat ourselves up, but turn to the Lord and believe it. We don't need to stay there for ANY reason, but we need to move ahead in the love and mercy of God. The Psalmist even says to be glad, rejoice and shout!! Could it be that simple or easy?

Psalm 32:10-11 *Many sorrows shall be to the wicked: but he that trusteth in the LORD, mercy shall compass him about. Be glad in the LORD, and rejoice, ye righteous: and shout for joy, all ye that are upright in heart.*

And lastly, to reiterate, we see that it is God's goodness that leads us to repentance. Don't ever try to beg people to repent, or tell them if they don't, God is going to get them or any other non-biblical tactic. It simply doesn't line up with the way God does things.

Romans 2:4 *Or despisest thou the riches of his goodness and forbearance and longsuffering; not knowing that the goodness of God leadeth thee to repentance?*

It really just doesn't get any better then this!! God is good.

Happy Freedom Day!

Keep Walking...

Stop Waiting

I want to return to the topic of self-effort and, once again, see how much God is against that.

If you read Isaiah Chapter 30, you will see that the Israelites were being rebellious children—sound familiar?? In verse three, you will see that they were trusting in the strength of something besides God. In this case it was Pharaoh.

Isaiah 30:1 *Woe to the rebellious children, saith the LORD, that take counsel, but not of me; and that cover with a covering, but not of my spirit, that they may add sin to sin:*

Isaiah 30:3 *Therefore shall the strength of Pharaoh be your shame, and the trust in the shadow of Egypt your confusion.*

It is pretty clear that if we are not trusting in God, then shame and confusion are allowed to manifest in our lives. I continue in my sometimes dyslexic style, i.e., look at it backwards. For example, if you have confusion in your life look at what/whom you might be trusting in—besides God! Why would we have confusion? Because we say one thing and do another. We say "I trust you God" and then rely on ourselves or other vain idols to help us.

Isaiah 30:15-16 *For thus saith the Lord GOD, the Holy One of Israel; In returning and rest shall ye be saved; in quietness and in confidence shall be your strength: and ye would not. But ye said, No; for we will flee upon horses; therefore shall ye flee: and, We will ride upon the swift; therefore shall they that pursue you be swift.*

I find this to be a very interesting passage. Basically God is telling them to repent, which in its most basic effort, means to change your mind.

We often say you need to turn and go the other direction, but if you weren't going in the right direction

Keep Walking..

to start with, turning will not necessarily take you on the right path!

Verse 15, very succinctly tells then "how" to repent, and to say the least, it is not how we usually do it. God is saying to do it in rest, confidence and quietness. A rest, that He already has forgiven them. Why? Because they are His people whom He would just really enjoy if they would serve Him. A confidence, because He is whom He says He is and keeps all of His promises. A quietness because God is amazingly profound and we need to be humble to receive the mightiness of His work; receptively and quietly.

Isaiah goes on to say that the people thought they would try their own self-effort plan. They thought that instead of trusting God, they would pick the strongest, fastest horses and flee. We will flee, we will ride - we, we, we all the way home!

Now look at God's awesome promise

Isaiah 30:18 *And therefore will the LORD wait, that he may be gracious unto you, and therefore will he be exalted, that he may have mercy upon you: for the LORD is a God of judgment: blessed are all they that wait for him.*

You know it's not nice to keep people waiting. Don't make God wait any longer for all of you!! I encourage you to read all of Isaiah Chapter 30.

Keep walking...

SIMPLE DELIVERANCE

A beautiful good morning to you! I am struck today by the simple things that God allows, to do mighty things. I encourage you to read all of 1Kings 19 of the story of Elijah running away from Jezebel—which by the way was a great thing to do!!

I am going to pull a few parts of the chapter to express what God was showing me this morning.

1 Kings 19:4 *But he himself went a day's journey into the wilderness, and came and sat down under a juniper tree: and he requested for himself that he might die; and said, It is enough; now, O LORD, take away my life;*

Have you ever felt like you were just done? Elijah was disappointed in his great work for God. Remember he had just called down fire from heaven, prayed in a bunch of needed rain and **1 Kings 18:46** says, *"and the hand of the Lord was on Elijah."*

1 Kings 19:10 continues saying that he ran away from Jezebel and the children of Israel had forsaken God's covenant.

In his mind, he had gone from being a chosen vessel of God to running away and sitting under a juniper tree. I am sure we have all felt like we have disappointed God, ourselves and others, and put in a request to die. First of all, having dealt with suicide, I am so grateful Elijah put in a request to God, rather than depend on his own thoughts and plans. God had a much better solution.

1 Kings 19:5-7 *⁵And as he lay and slept under a juniper tree, behold, then an angel touched him, and said unto him, Arise and eat. ⁶And he looked, and, behold, there was a cake baken on the coals, and a cruse of water at his head. And he did eat and drink, and laid him down again. ⁷And the angel of the LORD came again the second*

Keep Walking..

time, and touched him, and said, Arise and eat; because the journey is too great for thee.

God had a simple answer - arise and eat... get some sleep... eat some more and then rest again. Really?? No thunderous words from heaven, no time out because we felt like we haven't done all we could to serve God, no chastisement from the throne? Nope - just eat and sleep and then do it again. God even provided a "practical" angel to serve him. And then God showed him something significant.

1 Kings 19:12 *And after the earthquake a fire; but the LORD was not in the fire: and after the fire a still small voice.*

God used a simple ordinary thing of eating and resting and then spoke in a quiet voice. Are we often feeling so condemned by the "wind" or the "earthquake?" That, by the way, can be destructive, thinking we have failed to hear God. God is not here to punish and condemn us but to gently nurture us back to Him.

If you "need" a song to help you with this, please take a minute to listen to "You Deliver Me" by Selah Worship. Somehow it seems appropriate for Elijah's circumstances and ours as well. I hope it blesses you!

Keep walking...

CELEBRATING LOSS

Today would have been my son—Dustin's—thirtieth birthday. I choose to rejoice this day because God has made it. Many people ask how I manage to live a joyful life after losing my children in such tragic ways. I promise you, the ONLY way I do it is to rely on what God reminds me of in His Word.

Hebrews 11:13-16 *13These all died in faith, not having received the promises, but having seen them afar off, and were persuaded of them, and embraced them, and confessed that they were strangers and pilgrims on the earth. 14For they that say such things declare plainly that they seek a country. 15And truly, if they had been mindful of that country from whence they came out, they might have had opportunity to have returned. 16But now they desire a better country, that is, an heavenly: wherefore God is not ashamed to be called their God: for he hath prepared for them a city.*

This is a very meaningful passage to me. The first question you have to ask yourself is do you believe ALL of God's promises are "yes and amen"? And I mean every promise... healing for that sick friend, provision for your family, peace on earth, restoration of relationships, deliverance for that drug addicted child and the list goes on. That was my crossroads to fully embracing ALL of God, not just the part I wanted. I DID believe in healing, I did understand all that Jesus did on the cross and yet my son died, even after he had gotten saved in the hospital. I didn't understand. But the message in the passage does.

Many of us never see the answer to our prayer. That drug addicted child overdoses, the sick family member dies, you file bankruptcy, you are anxious and worried about the news, even after our faithful prayers. Don't worry, you are in good company. Go back and read all of Hebrews 11. These were mighty men and women of

Keep Walking..

God and they died not receiving the promise. You could stop there and be totally bummed out. Read the same passage in the Amplified version:

Hebrews 11:13-16 (Amplified) *¹³These people all died controlled and sustained by their faith, but not having received the tangible fulfillment of (God's) promises, only having seen it and greeting from a great distance by faith, and all the while acknowledging and confessing that they were strangers and temporary residents and exiles upon the earth. ¹⁴Now those people who talk as they did show plainly that they are in search of a fatherland (their own country). ¹⁵If they had been thinking with (homesick) remembrance of that country from which they were emigrants, they would have found constant opportunity to return to it. ¹⁶But the truth is that they were yearning for and aspiring to a better and more desirable country, that is, a heavenly (one). For that reason God is not ashamed to be called their God...for He has prepared a city for them.*

Do I prefer my old life or do I prefer to believe, embrace and confess the promises of God? If I do, I receive a whole city with my loved ones...and that is not only my children and family, but you, the family of God. I am standing on the promises! See you in our new country - it's going to be great!

Keep walking...

This One Thing

Happy almost lighter evenings!! I have had a wonderful time in Virginia and Colorado in all of the snow and zero degree weather, but I am definitely ready for some sunshine, warmth and longer evenings!!

Most of you know, I didn't graduate as a PhD in Pollyanism. I have many regrets as I am sure you do. In fact I have regrets over things as recently as an hour ago with a snide remark that was simply just that ...snide and unnecessary. Somehow, my flesh seems to be screaming at me and everyone else lately. That would have used to throw me in a whole self-hatred, I'm no good mode, that would then require self medication. Right now, I am banking on Paul's words.

Philippians 3:13-14 *Brethren, I count not myself to have apprehended: but this one thing I do, forgetting those things which are behind, and reaching forth unto those things which are before, I press toward the mark for the prize of the high calling of God in Christ Jesus.*

In Mary Pat language, that says to me, that I may dabble here and there and do some weird stuff, BUT THE ONE THING, is to forget that which I just did and press toward what God would desire in me... IN Jesus.

There are three parts to this "one thing." First, I have to forgive myself and forget the ground I have already covered in this race called life. I cannot waste time over the past. Not even the last five minutes. I used to be a runner, and I never once when running, thought about the steps I had already taken, it was what was ahead that was on the forefront of my mind.

The second thing, is that my future depends on not looking back. I am running for my life. I am hopefully moving forward in what God has perfectly ordained "in

Christ Jesus." God certainly knows I am not perfect and of course that is why He said "in Jesus" could I be perfected in this race a little more and more each day. Molding a lump of stubborn clay (me) never goes backwards. You may start over, but you don't do the same thing you just did. You throw it on the wheel, beat on it a little, smooth the rough edges with those loving hands, and bit by bit you make a nice something that you wanted. God is doing the same thing with you and me.

Lastly, we press toward the mark, the white line in the stadium, upon which each runner must keep their eyes fixed, less you be disqualified for the prize.

1 Corinthians 9:24-25 *Know ye not that they which run in a race run all, but one receiveth the prize? So run, that ye may obtain. And every man that striveth for the mastery is temperate in all things. Now they do it to obtain a corruptible crown; but we an incorruptible.*

I don't know your regrets, I only know mine. Thinking about these regrets hindering me from obtaining that incorruptible crown. Please take a minute and focus on "the one thing"—quit looking back, quit allowing the enemy to remind you of your past, even that snide remark five minutes ago. Ask for forgiveness, ask God to help you diminish that flesh and then of course it is up to us to "just do it." Duck tape works nicely too!

Keep running...

In Christ

We have been teaching, talking, meditating, chewing and trying to swallow the fullness of the Word in regards to the subject "In Christ." We have looked at many scriptures on the subject, starting with the foundation of Paul's letter to the Colossians.

Colossians 1:27 *To whom God would make known what is the riches of the glory of this mystery among the Gentiles; which is Christ in you, the hope of glory:*

We have dissected the word "mystery" which is defined as a secret that is known only to the initiated and requires special revelation. In the world we think of rituals found in cults, gangs etc., that are only known to the members. In the Bible, the mystery is the Church. Paul is in prison writing Ephesians, Colossians, Philippians and Philemon, and God is unfolding to him, the revelation of the church.

Ephesians 1:9-10 *Having made known unto us the mystery of his will, according to his good pleasure which he hath purposed in himself: That in the dispensation of the fulness of times he might gather together in one all things in Christ, both which are in heaven, and which are on earth; even in him:*

Next, we tackled, and struggled, I might add, with the topic statement of us as believers actually being "in Christ." We found that it means in union with, in mind, purpose and life—like a really great marriage! "In Christ" is a fixed position in rest. As a believer, the triune God imparts or discloses the mystery of being "in Him." This topic is almost overwhelming to us when we really realize that it is not who we are, but who we are in! If we are "in Him and He in us" then all fear should dissolve, our confidence should soar and we can get on with the business of fully representing Him in the world.

If "Perfect Love" lives in us, and love never fails, then Love, "in us," can conquer anything (**1 John 4:18, 1 Corinthians 13:8**).

Our next challenge in this topic, as we walk through the seemingly difficult situations of life, is to sit back and allow our eyes to see through His eyes in us. We see things through our own selfish desires and we often pray accordingly. These prayers may be really good, but when God answers them in a different way, we can get upset and begin to doubt how God's love and His care for us is possible. We are looking through our eyes only.

My challenge to you and me is to look at every situation that comes, whether it be at the store, in your family life, your job etc., and allow your eyes to see through the eyes of Christ. His is a different perspective. God's answer is not all about you and your needs, but the full work that He is trying to do on the earth through you.

Some of you know that I lost my two sons and mother several years ago. This was not the answer to my prayer!! However I trust that God has a different plan and He alone can take evil and turn it to good (Gen. 50:20). If I can separate myself from the selfishness of wanting my boys for me and trust God that He alone can use this to do a deep and powerful work in the earth, then the comfort of the Holy Spirit rises in my soul and releases me to fully submit all that I am and all that I have to the work of God.

And if you don't mind, I want to share this song again. Pay close attention to the third verse:

"Lifted up on Your shoulders, I'm a child once more From your higher perspective, showing me what's in store My realities changing, I'm seeing my life through Your eyes, Your eyes And all that You have given has taken my heart by surprise, by surprise."

"Lord, help us to trust You no matter what, and in the end, because we never doubted Your work on this earth,

Keep Walking...

that our hearts are surprised by all that You were able to do through Your's and our faithfulness."

Keep seeing...

(Song - Nicole Binion - Receive)

GOT JOY?

I am reminded of the verse in a song that says, "everyday in You, Lord, is better than the day before." I so agree with this, no matter what is going on at the time.

One day, Rick seemed somewhat quiet and subdued. I asked him where his joy was and his answer surprised me. He said "I don't have any, but the joy of the Lord is in me." That statement stopped me in my tracks, especially for him to say he didn't have any joy. That showed me a whole new layer of Christ living in me, and I in Him.

John 14:19-21 *Yet a little while, and the world seeth me no more; but ye see me: because I live, ye shall live also. At that day ye shall know that I am in my Father, and ye in me, and I in you. He that hath my commandments, and keepeth them, he it is that loveth me: and he that loveth me shall be loved of my Father, and I will love him, and will manifest myself to him.*

To be honest, of myself, I really don't have joy, or peace, or faith, or hope for the future. But, when I accept and believe "He in me," I have fullness of joy, fullness of the peace that passes all understanding, and fullness of faith and hope that the future is very bright.

It sure takes a lot of pressure off me trying to pull myself up by my bootstraps and be joyful, be righteous, be victorious, be healed and all the other attributes that are a part of who Jesus is. Instead, I can acknowledge that, of myself, I am nothing. I can acknowledge that "He in me" is all that I need, and I can allow Him to manifest Himself through me. Christ lives in me and is my Peace, my Healer, and my Righteousness, so I am just going to join Him in this intimate arrangement. I don't need to seek peace or healing; Jehovah Shalom and Jehovah Rapha live in me! This Truth will make you free!!

Keep Walking...

1 Corinthians 2:2 *For I determined not to know any thing among you, save Jesus Christ, and Him crucified.*

What if, no matter what we are learning from the scriptures, that at the end of the day we come back to "Christ crucified?" All our answers are right there. If there was no "Christ crucified," there would be no Peace, Righteousness, Healing, Provision and Victory. Ask yourself if you are willing to be "determined not to know anything" save Jesus Christ and Him crucified.

Keep digging...

Saving the Best for Last

I want to try and weave two great principles that I see in the Word. I have talked about them many times but found some new scriptures that continue to increase my faith in God's best. One thing that I continue to see is that we need to learn to look at things from God's perspective. If you know and trust Him, He will give you glimpses of His "higher" ways.

Matthew 16:21 *From that time forth began Jesus to shew unto his disciples, how that he must go unto Jerusalem, and suffer many things of the elders and chief priests and scribes, and be killed, and be raised again the third day.*

This verse comes after Peter had confessed Jesus as the Christ (Matthew 16:16). Now if we look at this statement of suffering, killing and then being raised again, it looks like a really bad deal for this so-called Son of God, called to be the King. That's because we look at it from our perspective. Suffering and being killed are not statements we like to hear from God. However, He had a greater purpose.

Hebrews 9:15-17 *[15]And for this cause he is the mediator of the new testament, that by means of death, for the redemption of the transgressions that were under the first testament, they which are called might receive the promise of eternal inheritance. [16]For where a testament is, there must also of necessity be the death of the testator. [17]For a testament is of force after men are dead: otherwise it is of no strength at all while the testator liveth.*

From God's point of view, suffering and death is what released us from the old covenant of the law into the new covenant of grace. Jesus HAD to die in order for our "benefits" to come forth. If you are going to receive something from someone's will, you will not get it until they die.

Keep Walking...

When Jesus died, His last will and testament (the Bible) and all His promises became ours. In other words, as I emphasize often, "The end of a thing is better than the beginning." (Eccl 7:8). If you are going through a tough time, know that, with Jesus, the end will be better. We see this principle at the wedding where He turned water into wine. Even the wedding guests noticed His unusual ways.

John 2:10-11 *¹⁰And saith unto him, Every man at the beginning doth set forth good wine; and when men have well drunk, then that which is worse: but thou hast kept the good wine until now. ¹¹This beginning of miracles did Jesus in Cana of Galilee, and manifested forth his glory; and his disciples believed on him.*

If you are "in Christ," I encourage you to try to trust God now more than ever. When things look so dark, and so bleak, you can encourage yourself with His ways. He always saves the best for last. You never need to despair if you know Him!!

Looking forward...

Got That Fire?

My question for you today is, "Who inspires you?" We see in 2 Thessalonians that Paul was inspired by the Thessalonians' patience and faith.

2 Thessalonians 1:3-7 *We are bound to thank God always for you, brethren, as it is meet, because that your faith groweth exceedingly, and the charity of every one of you all toward each other aboundeth; So that we ourselves glory in you in the churches of God for your patience and faith in all your persecutions and tribulations that ye endure: Which is a manifest token of the righteous judgment of God, that ye may be counted worthy of the kingdom of God, for which ye also suffer: Seeing it is a righteous thing with God to recompense tribulation to them that trouble you; And to you who are troubled rest with us, when the Lord Jesus shall be revealed from heaven with his mighty angels.*

It is quite inspiring to see that the Thessalonians are increasing in faith and love while bravely enduring persecution. It is clear evidence that God is at work preparing them for His kingdom. One day the present situation will be reversed, for the persecutors will themselves suffer tribulation and the persecuted will find rest when Christ returns.

Paul was inspired by their faithfulness and spiritual growth in hard times. Could someone be looking at you and be inspired as you go through tough situations? That is true evangelism. The words of the Jamie Grace/Jason Crabb song entitled "Fighter" remind me that no matter what, we need to be spiritually "large" in Him. Following are the words from the chorus that I hope will play through your head when you need Him most to keep going:

Keep Walking...

"He's a fighter, got that fire when they thought he'd fade away. Throws a fist up, as he gets up, feelin' stronger everyday When he gets down on his knees, he finds the courage to believe.

He's a fighter, he's a fighter who inspires me." Never, ever give up. Run the race...the reward will be waiting!

Keep running...

(Songs - Fighter - Acoustic feat and Jason Crabb - Jamie Grace - Ready to Fly)

JUST A TREE

Thank you for everyone who has dedicated a minute to read this message. None of you are insignificant to me or the kingdom work.

I am amazed at how the least significant thing we might do or say can make such a huge difference in someone's life and we never even know it. The devil takes a distinct advantage in this situation and tells you that you don't really do much for God in your day to day life, and loves to compare you to others. I don't know about you, but I try to keep my head above water just taking care of family, farm, work and the other necessary things that crowd our days. I often feel that I just don't do enough because I am thinking that I have to realize the significance! In reality, the most insignificant thing is probably the most powerful.

I am thinking of a simple tree. I mean just a tree, just seemingly like a million other trees. Sure, it tried to absorb water when it rained, it pushed it's roots down, it produced leaves in the spring and color came in the fall. It even remembered to shed it's leaves in the winter. Yep —the day in and day out stuff... ordinary... not very significant... just like the other trees. That is how most of us feel.

We know that simple insignificant tree was being prepared in a mighty way even during the seemingly dull days of just trying to keep upright and not fall over (sound familiar?). The tree didn't know that it was being prepared to bear a Savior. Soon it would be part of a much greater plan for love for all.

What if God is doing the same in us, when the days just seem to slip by? As we live in a routine that never seems to allow us to "do the things for God," we need to consider that God Himself might just be preparing

Keep Walking...

us for something significant in His eyes that allows Him to accomplish His will. We always think we have to "do something" in order to get God to move. I hate to break it to you, but God has already done everything you and I need. We don't have to sing in the choir, teach Sunday School and volunteer for every event in order for God to heal us, mend our marriage, get us a good job or fill in the blank. We need to appropriate all that He has already done, when He said "it is finished."

I am sure that tree never had any idea that by being available in God's time table, that all of mankind could be redeemed.

There are 201 verses containing the word "tree." It started with a tree, we got saved because of a tree; we get healing, peace, provision, and victory in our own earthly lives because of a tree, and finally life will be eternal and full because of a tree.

Revelation 22:2 *In the midst of the street of it, and on either side of the river, was there the tree of life, which bare twelve manner of fruits, and yielded her fruit every month: and the leaves of the tree were for the healing of the nations.*

Revelation 22:14 *Blessed are they that do his commandments, that they may have right to the tree of life, and may enter in through the gates into the city.*

If you know me, you know I love music. It often speaks to me in a way words don't. If you have an extra minute, enjoy the "tree" song.

No matter what, you are not insignificant. As a matter of a fact, God might just surprise you.

(Song - Shadow Of A Tree – Shannon Wexelberg)

Be surprised (I know that tree was!).

Even as He Walked

I am on my "walking" thing again, so you might as well put on your walking shoes and go with me.

1 John 2:6 *He that saith he abideth in him ought himself also so to walk, even as he walked.*

Most of us are pretty proud that we are walking with Him especially through trying times. The part we may be unsure of is the "even as He walked." Often as we deal with unpleasant situations, we are proud of our prayers and our time spent with Him and the wonderful outcome that reminds us of God's greatness and heart towards us. But we sometimes have to lean into more difficult callings and that is to walk even as He walked. We are not too sure about this word "even." God gives us His way:

Psalm 84:5-7 *Blessed is the man whose strength is in thee; in whose heart are the ways of them. Who passing through the valley of Baca make it a well; the rain also filleth the pools. They go from strength to strength, every one of them in Zion appeareth before God.*

We may be called to walk through the valley of Baca. Baca is a type of plant that can survive in dry conditions. The cool word here is "survive" and then passing through. Those of us who really trust in God can pass through and survive the driest times, because we "make it a well." We trust in God's strength and not our own. We can go from strength to strength which each step taken.

That's all I want to say.

If God's and my voice ever ring together in your head, please hear "keep walking."

There is a river whose streams make glad!!

With a most profound love...

Keep Walking...

Faith Versus Senses

I hope you are enjoying the senses God gave you to enjoy the spring awakening. God gave us the use of sight, smell, hearing, tasting and touch to function in this world. God's plan for using my senses as a Christian has made a profound impact on my life.

2 Corinthians 5:7 *(For we walk by faith, not by sight:)*

Over the last years, if I had to walk by what was going on around me, I know I would have sunk to the lowest of despair. God is telling me NOT to use my sense of sight, but instead believe in His promises. I chose to look up and not around, in order to keep walking in faith.

Romans 10:17 *So then faith cometh by hearing, and hearing by the word of God.*

We now have another scripture that says to use our sense of hearing to increase our faith. God began to show me that yes, our senses are for use in this world, but we have to determine the correct combination. Our worldly senses plus the Holy Spirit can move us in this walk of faith. If we take our physical senses, plus a spirit that is not of God, such as fear, then we will have fear influencing everything that our senses pick up. If we combine our senses with the Holy Spirit then we find the advantage of this scripture:

Hebrews 5:14 *But strong meat belongeth to them that are of full age, even those who by reason of use have their senses exercised to discern both good and evil.*

We gather information through our natural senses, but then we "walk by faith, not by sight." We take in our environment, but then have to decide if it is going to dictate our lives or if we are going to walk by something we cannot see, but have read in the Word, as a promise of God.

Keep Walking..

In summary, God gave us our senses to use in the natural world. If we combine that with the Holy Spirit to use in discernment, then we can choose God's way. If we choose the natural way, I am afraid we may sink. Remember when Peter was walking on water? The waves and the wind were just as high and strong when he was walking as when he began to sink. The difference initially was that he was walking by faith, not by sight.

This walk in life requires a lifting of your head, and your hands. Look up not around, and you may find that things are going to be just fine. Our worldly senses, without God, can destroy us. Walk in faith, hands raised, and head up!

Onward Christian Soldier!

A Scent of Water

Many of you have been "walking" with me for a long time and I am grateful for the relationships that have been built through all this exercise! Lately I seem to be stuck on "water." Over and over again, I hear in my head, the simple phrase, "there is a river." I feel like I have been in a dry spell lately, so maybe God is showing me to embrace the Water.

I was listening to a preacher this morning and this scripture came up. It encouraged me as I really felt like I didn't have anything but desert dust to write about, and that certainly did not interest me!

Job 14:7-9 *For there is hope of a tree, if it be cut down, that it will sprout again, and that the tender branch thereof will not cease. Though the root thereof wax old in the earth, and the stock thereof die in the ground; Yet through the scent of water it will bud, and bring forth boughs like a plant.*

We can apply this to our own lives. Maybe we feel cut down, cut off, and losing our vibrant life. Lately, I have felt just that...but "there is a River!" We see the "tree" above cut off from its source of life, it's roots, and there seems to be no hope other than a future life of decay. But hallelujah, there is a "scent" of water. That excites me! Not a big dowsing of water or submerging into cool refreshment, but a scent. The Hebrew language describes it as an "odor as if blown."

If we don't feel like we have the spiritual energy to jump in the Living Water to become revived, the Word says if we can just get close enough, we can have hope of budding again. I am amazed at how little the Lord expects of us and how powerfully significant He can be in our lives if we allow it.

Keep Walking..

Let's look at this scripture from another perspective. The "tree" that held Jesus was cut down and everyone thought it was over. But the "scent" of Living Water resurrected Him to full life. Not just for Him but for us all.

I don't know where you are today, but I know that this newsletter was for me. I just needed a scent of Water to revive me again.

Get near the Water...

Keep Walking...

WHY GOD?

I know many times we ask God "why" and feel like we are getting the silent treatment. We may ask things like, "Why can't You just tell us what is going on so we can understand and figure it out?" I heard this question recently, "Why would we want to serve a God we can fully understand?" If my little peanut brain can figure God out, I don't really need to come talk to Him, as I already know what He is going to say or do. If I can understand all that God does, then He is probably really not that big.

We know God's thoughts and ways are higher than ours and so much infinitely bigger and better! (Isaiah 55:8-9) But, we still want to ask Him over and over, "Why?" For an atheist, the question "Why?" has no meaning; for a believer the question "Why?" finds its ultimate answer in God. In the midst of our situation, can we believe that all of God's promises are yes and amen? (2Cor 1:20)

If you read the book of Habakkuk, you will find God's simple, but profound, answer. A quick overview of this book shows that Habakkuk lived during a period when the country was at its worst. There was violence, oppression, and collapse of the legal system. There was war all around. Habakkuk addresses God, although he really believed God had removed Himself from the earthly scene. This book gives the account of a spiritual journey, telling of one man's pilgrimage from doubt to worship.

Habakkuk 2:3 *For the vision is yet for an appointed time, but at the end it shall speak, and not lie: though it tarry, wait for it; because it will surely come, it will not tarry.*

In the midst of the storm, with Habakkuk crying out to a seemingly silent God, who won't give him the answer to his "why" questions, the Lord simply says:

Keep Walking..

Habakkuk 2:4 *But the just shall live by his faith.*

"Shall live" in the Hebrew language means to be preserved, to flourish, to enjoy life, to live in happiness, to breath, be animated (love that one), to recover health, etc. Of course if you are a believer, you are the "just." All the garbage from your past is "just like" it didn't happen. Paul reiterates that point:

Romans 1:16-17 *For I am not ashamed of the gospel of Christ: for it is the power of God unto salvation to everyone that believeth; to the Jew first, and also to the Greek. For therein is the righteousness of God revealed from faith to faith: as it is written, The just shall live by faith.*

And while I am on a scripture roll, I encourage you to read this aloud! It is the passing of Habakkuk from doubt to worship. May you pass along that route as well!

Habakkuk 3:17-19 *Although the fig tree shall not blossom, neither shall fruit be in the vines; the labour of the olive shall fail, and the fields shall yield no meat; the flock shall be cut off from the fold, and there shall be no herd in the stalls: Yet I will rejoice in the LORD, I will joy in the God of my salvation. The LORD God is my strength, and he will make my feet like hinds' feet, and he will make me to walk upon mine high places. To the chief singer on my stringed instruments.*

Big hugs!

Encouraged in the Silence

I wonder if you trust that you are being led by God? Many of you know that I have started a new job, one which I really didn't qualify for at all, but yet, was quickly hired. I just completed 80 hours of training and, once again, with God's favor, passed the competency test with flying colors. I also have an "A" in my Anatomy and Physiology classes.

The reason I tell you this is that my memory has never been good. This is due to poor choices growing up, i.e., drugs, which makes it tough to retain new and challenging information without studying for hours. But with God's grace, and my belief that this is His will for my life, I am able to remember and retain all this knowledge without studying too much. I keep telling Him, and reminding myself, that if He wants me to be doing this, then He is responsible for getting me through!

You may also remember that I thought I would probably have to stop writing the newsletter, limit doing the conference call and maybe quit the Bible study I do in town. God has allowed me to keep up with all these activities without a lot of stress. Somehow, He gives me the time to do everything He wants me to do. I am excited to see what God is going to do with a 57 year old women in the medical field. I so feel this is not about me. I have had the "big career" and life is good on the farm, but yet I have felt so led to take on these new things! If nothing else, my brain is getting the workout of a lifetime!!

With all that said, I would like to say a few more things that E. Stanley Jones talked about in his devotion book. He talks about "getting music out of life's remainders." It immediately made me think of Paul and Silas down in the dungeon singing their hearts out. It also made me think of the saying "making lemonade out of lemons."

First and foremost you need to know that God is IN your situation!! A believer should be one who, when he gets to the end of his rope, ties a knot and hangs on... the old "keep walking" thing.

Jones (Stanley - not Rick or me) shares about the "silence in heaven about the space of half an hour," spoken of in Revelation. Read closely and you will see that God was shifting the scenes for the next act.

Revelations 8:1-4 *And when he had opened the seventh seal, there was silence in heaven about the space of half an hour. And I saw the seven angels which stood before God; and to them were given seven trumpets. And another angel came and stood at the altar, having a golden censer; and there was given unto him much incense, that he should offer it with the prayers of all saints upon the golden altar which was before the throne. And the smoke of the incense, which came with the prayers of the saints, ascended up before God out of the angel's hand.*

The silent, suffering spaces in your life may be God getting you ready for the next, great act.

Hold steady, the next act will come. In the meantime, take hold of your dull drab moments, your worst situation and make them give forth music.

Can we find our joy in the silence when we feel like God went on vacation? Can we sit back and only imagine what God is doing in our worst situation, knowing that He will never leave us or forsake us, and His plan will be the best we could ever put together? Can we wait in the silence knowing that our prayers are going up like incense to the Lord? Can we remember that Jesus says that nothing outside a man can defile him... it is what comes from within defiles him? (Mark 17:15) Your outside situation cannot defile or hurt you. It is your attitude, words and actions that predict the outcome. Pain is inevitable, overcoming is optional.

Keep Walking...

1 John 5:4-5 *For whatsoever is born of God overcometh the world: and this is the victory that overcometh the world, even our faith. Who is he that overcometh the world, but he that believeth that Jesus is the Son of God?*

Be born of God, be an overcomer, be encouraged in the silence and of course

Keep walking...

ONE TITLE

I have one simple message today and it is something very humbling to ponder. Again, I am sharing some material from the E. Stanley Jones devotional. He makes the statement "Don't try to be a leader - be the servant of all and out of that service you will gain leadership as a byproduct. The attitude of a leader is "I lead, you follow," it is self assertive and thus cannot be Christianized." He then goes on to say that Jesus said there was only one title He could trust us with and that is the title of "servant."

That got my attention and made me realize how right He is. Whether I give myself the title of doctor, lawyer, president or a person with cancer, disease, devastated, traumatized, angry, rejected, guilty and so on, I must go back to the only title that Jesus suggests that I be called—a servant. It makes me realize the power of that single title and the importance of doing away with all the other ones that we may have given ourselves or have had pronounced over us through a lifetime.

Matthew 23:10-11 *Neither be ye called masters: for one is your Master, even Christ. But he that is greatest among you shall be your servant.*

Jesus trusts us with one title. Let's try to live that one and that one alone. The simplicity of the Gospel is more profound than anything we can imagine. Go ahead and try!!

Keep walking...

A Good Soldier

HI am most thankful that I know, beyond a shadow of doubt, who Jesus is in my life. I don't know about Him, I know Him. There is a huge difference; the difference between religion and relationship and between happiness and joy. Knowing Him is real, it is hopeful and most of all it is everlasting!

After Thanksgiving we will be going back and studying the "No Shuffling, No Pink Fuzzy Slippers" teaching which is really about going through tough times with the grace and peace of God for all to see. We will be starting with this scripture, which is what it takes to be successful in God's eyes, not to mention a joyful peace in life on earth.

2 Timothy 2:3 *Thou therefore endure hardness, as a good soldier of Jesus Christ.*

The word "hardness" in the Greek is affliction. But the word that got my attention was "good." We think that "good" would mean a strong, courageous, enduring soldier. But good means beautiful, valuable or virtuous for appearance or use. God expects us to deal with afflictions with the beautiful, valuable, countenance of the grace of God that others will see. We should not be dressed up in self-pity of religious martyrdom but in radiant beauty.

If you are going through a tough time (or the next time you do), is your face beautiful and glowing with the grace that only God can provide? If not, I have a friend that says "talk to your face!" Remind your face of the only one who can deliver and minister to you during your greatest trial. Preach the gospel to your face! God says He will provide His grace in "our time of need," not all the time, but in our time of greatest suffering. You might just find that the trial is teaching you something about the good-

Keep Walking..

ness of the one, true, Living God and how, through the trial, He is answering your prayer to be more like Him. Sometimes it takes a little chiseling.

Happy Thanksgiving to all the good soldiers out there!.

Big hugs...

Chosen and Ordained

It truly is a time of new seasons for me and I am sure for you as well. We know that no matter what, seasons always change!

Let's look at Paul's words:

1 Corinthians 2:4-5 *And my speech and my preaching was not with enticing words of man's wisdom, but in demonstration of the Spirit and of power: That your faith should not stand in the wisdom of men, but in the power of God.*

Lately I have had difficulty with all the media world stuff we find in the Christian "scene." Maybe it is time to get away from all the fancy production and latest media whiz and just look at the Word in simple black and white. Really that is what it is... simple but life changing... totally effective on its own... that sharp two-edged sword that does the greatest surgery in our lives.

If we don't believe we are being led by the Holy Spirit, we will probably fall victim to our circumstances. Today I want to emphasize more truth of the Word, if we could only believe!

John 15:16 *Ye have not chosen me, but I have chosen you, and ordained you, that ye should go and bring forth fruit, and that your fruit should remain: that whatsoever ye shall ask of the Father in my name, he may give it you.*

In Jesus words, we did not "make" ourselves Christians, He did!! Not only that, HE has ordained us to go and bring forth fruit and it should remain as a legacy of Him in the earth.

Not only did He choose us, but He ordained us. The word ordained in the Greek means to place in an upright and active position. If Jesus did that, then He has placed

Keep Walking..

us in an active position, upright, only because of our belief in Him, then how can we not accept that we are led by the Holy Spirit.

If I create a clock, I make it to work and tell time because of the purpose I desire. If God created us upright, active, ordained to bring forth fruit, then He will have to make it work as well.

As we walk through a new season, let us trust that Jesus has chosen us and ordained us to bring forth fruit. If you are feeling like you have had a major crop failure, then maybe Jesus has a different way to bring forth fruit. He makes it work.

One of the things I have really tried to focus on lately, is that if Jesus is with me and in me, then there is a blessing in it—no matter what the circumstances. My biggest prayer to God lately, is to help me see the blessing in this. I know it is there, because I know YOU are there and will never leave or forsake me. If that's the case, it's here somewhere and what a change this has made in my life.

Where is the blessing in your worst situation? Ask God to show it to you.

And as always, keep walking!

Not My Joy But His

Good morning to you all! I pray you are allowing God to do His great work in you. I promise it is easier when we allow Him to do the work, and be Himself in us!

John 15:9-11 *As the Father hath loved me, so have I loved you: continue ye in my love. If ye keep my commandments, ye shall abide in my love; even as I have kept my Father's commandments, and abide in his love. These things have I spoken unto you, that my joy might remain in you, and that your joy might be full.*

Do you see it? God tells us that it is love, love, love. God loves His Son, His Son loves us and we need to love each other. It isn't us trying to muster up some love to share with others, especially some in our paths, but it is a love waterfall from God flowing down. We just get dumped on with love if we allow it. If we receive His love, we want to serve Him and keep His commandments because we are so full of love. Don't you remember that first boyfriend or girlfriend? You just couldn't love and serve them enough. You always let them have their own way because the love was just so gushy. How much more should we be able to love, serve and esteem others higher than ourselves, with the love of God?

After God tells us about this love, He then tells us that His joy (Greek-calm delight) remains in us and should be full (Greek-replete; to cram). I can't seem to say this right so let me try again. It's HIS joy IN US. It is not up to me to muster up joy, but to receive His love poured out through Jesus, and allow that to incubate into a joyful heart.

God gets His greatest delight in us when we are joyful in Him. Rick's big revelation is that God is not interested so much in all our doings, but are we joyful? We are joyful because of love and, of course, love never fails

Keep Walking..

and, of course, God is love. People are always drawn to joy. God smiles.

I pray for each of you that happiness is not the goal, but joy. Joy is real, it is authentically from God, and it is powerful. And as Rick says, "God smiles at His joy that we allow to manifest in us, even in difficult times." Joy is because of love and love is because of Jesus. If you are born again, there is no reason you should not be joyful.

Find Him, find joy!

Keep Walking...

We Want What We Want

Joyful day to you all. I am trying to get rid of the "happy" word because it only lasts as long as my senses like what they see and hear. Joy is permanent, from Him and in Him. That is one thing I want forever in my life! Happy is from the world and certainly man-made. Why do we always seem to want what man has, versus what God has for us? I was reading in first Samuel and the problem was the same then as it is now.

1 Samuel 8:18-20 *And ye shall cry out in that day because of your king which ye shall have chosen you; and the LORD will not hear you in that day. Nevertheless the people refused to obey the voice of Samuel; and they said, Nay; but we will have a king over us; That we also may be like all the nations; and that our king may judge us, and go out before us, and fight our battles.*

Here we have Samuel, the last judge, telling the Israelites, who were wanting a king "like all the nations," that if they were going to chose a king, then the Lord would not hear them. But then you have the old "nevertheless" word-- which is kind of like our word "whatever" (said in our passive, we are not paying attention, attitude). What follows is a most profound statement of God. He is not going to listen to them if they refuse Him and desire a man to be their king. "People wake up now," you want to scream!!

The word "nation" in the Hebrew language, in this passage, means a foreign nation/heathens. God's very own people, the Jews, were telling God that they wanted to be like everyone else, they wanted to have a man fight their battles and judge them. You just want to shake your head and say, "Don't you remember Gideon's battle and many others where God purposefully made the Israelite army very small so they couldn't take any credit?"

God wanted to show them His great love and power over them if they would trust Him...nevertheless...

Jude 7:2 *And the LORD said unto Gideon, The people that are with thee are too many for me to give the Midianites into their hands, lest Israel vaunt themselves against me, saying, Mine own hand hath saved me.*

Sometimes I wonder if we are the dumbest species on earth. God is so good and yet we prefer our own strength, skills, talents and hard work. We trust ourselves more than we trust our own Father who created us and is sovereign over all. We always want to be our own savior, in essence saying, we don't need God.

Psalm 108:12-13 *Give us help from trouble: for vain is the help of man. Through God we shall do valiantly: for he it is that shall tread down our enemies.*

I will leave you alone now with one last question. Do you have an enemy in your life? It could be a failing marriage, a health problem, a problem with children or work or one of a million issues. I urge you to pray Psalm 108:12-13 over the situation and see what the King of Kings will do. I promise you it will be better than any counselor, any medicine or anything else the world offers.

Through God.

ONE ANSWER

Thank you so much for joining me as we dissect, tackle and build our faith as we study the book of Galatians. I never realized how much legalism still remained in my life until I began this journey. I have found a whole new level of freedom and I pray that you will too. My focus from this day forward is:

1 Corinthians 2:2 *For I determined not to know anything among you, save Jesus Christ, and him crucified.*

For every question, every situation, every loss, every disease, etc., there is one answer if I am willing to look at it... and it is... Christ crucified. Begin your own test with everything in your life and see if an answer has already been accomplished and finished by Him.

Of course you must "know" Him, and that intimate knowing comes from studying the scriptures.

John 19:30 *When Jesus therefore had received the vinegar, he said, It is finished: and he bowed his head, and gave up the ghost.*

To share my own situation, I received a call that my 58 year old sister had passed away. She was found in her apartment, apparently having died of an internal bleed. I have learned a lot about death and because of that I remained "steady." The Bible says that Jesus took my grief and sorrows. My sister knew the Lord, although never allowed Him to take away the guilt from her past. Of course, I will greatly miss my sister, as I do my children and other family members, but I will see them again. It is not "good bye" but "see you later." I can handle that.

Isaiah 53:4 *Surely he hath borne our griefs, and carried our sorrows: yet we did esteem him stricken, smitten of God, and afflicted.*

Keep Walking..

I feel like God encouraged me with the following quote from a Beth Moore Bible study. "The power of the resurrection means that nothing but the tomb is meant to remain empty." With this new and fresh loss, I am able to go back to the tomb, where there is emptiness of this loss. I fill myself up with Him. That is how I choose to keep moving forward.

And lastly, a quote from the workbook that goes with the "No Shuffling, No Pink Fuzzy Slippers" teaching:

"For those who have welcomed Christ, the Risen Savior, into their life, you can welcome death, because in death there are no periods, only commas."

For all of this to work in your life, you must be born again. If you have been "agnostic" with worry and not trusting God in situations of your life, perhaps it is time to press in and know Him. Whatever I can do to help you move forward would be a privilege and honor. Let me know how I can best serve you!

John 3:3 *Jesus answered and said unto him, Verily, verily, I say unto thee, Except a man be born again, he cannot see the kingdom of God.*

Big hugs, walking and breathing.

Worry – A Kind of Atheism

I wanted to share a few thoughts on fear and worry. First of all, Christians need to expunge the word "worry" from their vocabulary. Worry or fear is a kind of atheism. It says that you cannot trust God and will take things into your own hands. The world favorably calls this "your independence and ability to take care of yourself." I call it stupid, having tried it my own way for so many years, and ending up pretty much dead.

Worry says that God doesn't care, He's too busy for me, He's not able, or His timetable doesn't fit with my needs. Faith says that God does care and that He and I will work it out together.

Matthew 8:26 *And he saith unto them, Why are ye fearful, O ye of little faith? Then he arose, and rebuked the winds and the sea; and there was a great calm.*

It is pretty clear here that lack of faith brings on the fear. Oswald Chambers puts it like this, "When we are afraid, the least we can do is pray. But our Lord has a right to expect that those who pray in His name have an underlying confidence in Him. God expects His children to be so confident in Him that in any crisis they are the ones who are reliable. Yet our trust is only in God up to a certain point, then we turn back to the elementary, panic stricken prayers of those people who do not even know God."

Fear brings out our independence, i.e., forget you God. We must have the breaking and collapse of our independence if we are going to be followers of Jesus Christ and live a life of faith. No one can do that for us. God may bring us up to this point, through situations derived to crush our own self efforts, but He cannot, and will not, push us through it. We must do it ourselves.

Keep Walking..

We must break that fortress of independence from God and choose absolute loyalty to Him.

Has that breaking of your independence come? All the rest is religious fraud. Oh, that hurts my pious, fabricated Christian identity. Will we surrender to Jesus Christ, placing no conditions whatsoever as to how the brokenness will come? When we reach the point of total dependence on Him, immediately the reality of the Spirit of God in me, the Great I AM, the completed works of Jesus Christ, can manifest in every area of our lives. We have truly been crucified with Christ. The most powerful word I know in the Greek, "crucified," means to extinguish selfishness. Lord, help me give up my independence, remind me daily that, if I don't, it is religious fraud. I don't want to hear those words..." depart from me..."

Luke 13:27 *But he shall say, I tell you, I know you not whence ye are; depart from me, all ye workers of iniquity.*

Galatians 2:20 *I am crucified with Christ: nevertheless I live; yet not I, but Christ liveth in me: and the life which I now live in the flesh I live by the faith of the Son of God, who loved me, and gave himself for me.*

It is time for an independent flesh fry!

Give it Up.

Keep Walking...

FRAGMENTS TO FEED OTHERS

My newsletters always seem to have the same ring and this one is no different. I just got excited about reading it in the Word from another angle.

John 6:11-12 *And Jesus took the loaves; and when he had given thanks, he distributed to the disciples, and the disciples to them that were set down; and likewise of the fishes as much as they would. When they were filled, he said unto his disciples, Gather up the fragments that remain, that nothing be lost.*

Oh wow—Jesus says, *"Gather up the fragments that nothing be lost."* Do you ever feel like you have some "fragments" out there? Maybe there are past regrets, hurts or losses that you can't even verbalize or put on paper, and here Jesus is saying to gather them up. Why in the world does He want fragments? From the five barley loaves and two small fishes, Jesus had fed every one and they were filled. Everything was good, now the disciples just needed to do a little clean up. Jesus said gather that "nothing be lost." The word "lost" means destroyed in the Greek language. He did not want the fragments of bread and fish or the fragments of our lives destroyed. Instead, He has a planned use for them.

The similar stories of feeding the multitudes with bread and fish (**Matthew 15:33** and **Mark 8:4**) say there were fragments left over also. The stories never tell us what happened to all the leftovers, but we know that God didn't want them thrown out.

Jesus is the Bread of Life, and every fragment of Him is useful to us for life on earth and for eternity. If we are "in Him" then the fragments of our lives are useful too. I believe the fragments are our testimony, and we know from Revelation that our testimonies defeat the devil.

Keep Walking..

Thus God didn't want the fragments "destroyed" but to be used for others.

When you restore an old car, you take ALL the parts; good, bad and ugly, and give them to the person who will restore the car. The bad parts are as valuable as the parts that are in much better shape. We have to use all the parts for the restoration. In our lives, we need to take the rusty, worn out, ugly parts, and let Him use and restore them. God wants all of us so He can restore us to the fullness of His image through Jesus and as a result help restore others. Our part?? Be willing to let it all go!! God uses fragments like we can never imagine!!

Gather the Fragments...

Drinking the New Wine

God inspires me! I love to write about it. There is nothing worse than trying to represent and stir up God in the flesh. Actually, it doesn't produce anything at all. It is like doing surgery with a foam scalpel versus the sharp two-edged sword of the Word. I pray that Proverbs speaks to you today and does a little surgery in your life that will bring great healing.

Proverbs 11:6 *The righteousness of the upright shall deliver them: but transgressors shall be taken in their own naughtiness.*

Proverbs 11:9 *An hypocrite with his mouth destroyeth his neighbour: but through knowledge shall the just be delivered.*

Proverbs is saying that our righteousness delivers us (vs 6) and that through knowledge the just shall be delivered (vs 9). This is an extremely simple concept. Righteousness and knowledge shall deliver us. We need to believe the Word, and if we do and if we are truly born again, then the knowledge that Jesus is our righteousness should help us walk in the deliverance that is already ours.

We have talked about the mixture of the law and grace and how nothing good comes out of it. If you put new wine (new covenant of grace) in old wine bottles (old covenant of law) then the wine is spilled out and the bottles break. Not a good rate of return on your investment! However the last scripture in that story confused me until I realized we "must be born again." (John 3:7 Marvel not that I said unto thee, Ye must be born again.)

Luke 5:39 *No man also having drunk old wine straightway desireth new: for he saith, The old is better.*

Keep Walking..

This is saying that if you are under the law and are comfortable in your own self-effort of "doing good," then you won't desire the new covenant of grace and you will just continue in your old ways. In other words, we like being in charge of us, and not depending on anyone or anything else. It is a false sense of control when we don't want to join ourselves to the gospel of grace and of being led by the Holy Spirit; of doing what God desires. We would just as soon depend on ourselves because we "know" what we are capable of doing (or so we think). We depend on the flesh—the law—to determine whether we think we are good or bad. It is exhausting.

I have a favorite saying and that is "we cling to known hell rather than move to unknown heaven." We can be familiar and pretty good at dealing with abusive marriages, dysfunction, diseases or financial trouble because that is what we know. We have learned how to cope on our own. We cling to that because we don't know what would happen if we let go of self- control and allow God in on our circumstances. We can't trust Him because we don't KNOW Him.

If we knew Him, we would know He has a far better way for us to live.

Gulp down the new wine.

Spirit Led

Several years ago I wanted to try and study what it meant to be led by the Spirit. After much human effort, God spoke to me and basically said, "You have no idea of the future, but if you will trust Me, it will be better than anything you can figure out." Being led by the Spirit means I have to trust that He has a purpose and plan that I am not necessarily privy to. Often, I don't like that!! But I do trust Him more than I trust myself. His track record is way better than mine.

I was reading a devotional the other day and a sentence jumped out at me. It said, "If we lose the sense of being led, we become victims of our circumstances." That can be so true. If I think I am on a road of random events, I will simply react in my own flesh to things going on. Or I can trust that God's ways are perfect and He is sanctifying me for His greatest purpose. With this, I can expect some fires along the way to burn up the dross that the generations and/or I have picked up along the way. The result can be the transformation of God in my life—what we are usually praying for anyway!!

I don't want situations, surroundings and flat out annoying people to make my day bad or life bad because it doesn't suit my fancy or fit into my plan. We cry out that we want God, and for Him to perfect us and heal us and deliver us and, and, etc. If we would realize, Jesus finished it ALL on the cross and that is what He wants as well, then maybe all these situations wouldn't bother us so much. We could see them for what they are worth. That worth is that God loves us enough to hear our prayers, and perfect, heal and deliver us in the way that will work—His way.

Keep Walking..

Luke 4:1 *And Jesus being full of the Holy Ghost returned from Jordan, and was led by the Spirit into the wilderness.*

Romans 8:14 *For as many as are led by the Spirit of God, they are the sons of God.*

Galatians 5:18 *But if ye be led of the Spirit, ye are not under the law.*

Learn to trust God and be led by His Holy Spirit so you don't have the "victim of my circumstances" mentality. I promise that life will be more adventuresome and less tormenting.

John 15:11 *These things have I spoken unto you, that my joy might remain in you, and that your joy might be full.*

It's His joy in us. Don't you think He has the best way to bring it forth? Be led by the Spirit and walk a life of faith.

"O God, we are so afraid to be led by your Holy Spirit and often are led by things and surrounding and other people. Our relationship with You becomes secondhand and vague, instead of firsthand and vibrant. Help us to regain the sense of being led, the sense that we are in direct contact and that life has its greatest meaning and worth when being led by You."

Lead on...

Keep Walking...

HE GOT UP!

Resurrection Day is approaching and it is very exciting to celebrate that Jesus "got up!" Nothing could keep Him down, and therefore, since He is our example, nothing should keep you down—at least not for long!!

Many of us are going through tough, burdensome times. Let's take a moment to visit Jesus in the garden of Gethsemane. He is getting ready to bear ALL of these sins (trauma, tragedy, sickness, shame, etc.) for us, and being a man, had the same response that I had several years ago, and perhaps you are having today.

Luke 22:42 *Saying, Father, if thou be willing, remove this cup from me: nevertheless not my will, but thine, be done.*

In our agony and concern over what is coming next, we cry out the first part of this plea, "Please take this from me." Could we, in our everyday life, always include the second part of this scripture... "nevertheless?" In my Webster 1937 dictionary, the word actually breaks down to "not the less." In this verse it is then followed by the word "not." What I hear the Spirit of the Lord saying is, "I see what you are going through and I know it seems overwhelming but "no, no, not the less" but My will, which is far greater and far more beneficial to you, be done. He is saying He wants His best for us. So often, we only see things through our own physical eyes, when if we could only look through the eyes of God, we could see all that He is doing. That still doesn't often comfort us. As I looked at the next verse, much comfort came.

Luke 22:43 *And there appeared an angel unto him from heaven, strengthening him.*

Whatever you are going through, have gone through, or will go through, know that in your weakest moment,

Keep Walking..

God sends an angel to strengthen you. We may not feel it or believe it for the moment, but I promise in that darkest time, you will be strengthened.

And lastly a quote from David Crowder (a Christian song artist) who is reflecting on this Resurrection season from his book, "Everybody wants to go to Heaven, but No One Wants to Die." It goes like this:

"Once a year I stand and sing in the knowledge that death doesn't win. And every single person we have loved and lost, who are missed and envied, you got there first!"

Remember the sting of death has been overcome. Watch the Lamb!

Keep watching...

WHY GOD?

As we reflect on the death and resurrection of Jesus, it brought to mind the question of "why God doesn't always heal." It seemed as though life for Jesus was over, just like it may seem that your own life will be over soon. You have done all that you know to do to touch God's heart for your healing and yet it seems like He went on a shopping spree and forgot to listen... "nevertheless" (remember last message, "no, not the less?").

We can look at the life of Paul where he healed many just with "handkerchiefs and aprons" (Act 19:12). It looks like he had it going on in the healing department. But read the following written by Paul:

2 Timothy 4:20 *Erastus abode at Corinth: but Trophimus have I left at Miletum sick.*

Trophimus was an Ephesian who had traveled with Paul on his third missionary journey. Paul left him behind sick, expresses an enigma concerning healing. He himself—a man who operated in divine healing—was not able to heal his own issues.

2 Corinthians 12:8 *For this thing I besought the Lord thrice, that it might depart from me.*

2 Corinthians 12:9 *And he said unto me, My grace is sufficient for thee: for my strength is made perfect in weakness. Most gladly therefore will I rather glory in my infirmities, that the power of Christ may rest upon me.*

Although divine healing is a promised part of the saint's inheritance, sometimes we are not healed, even when we have prayed in faith and confessed our faith outwardly. The Bible does not give explicit answers to this puzzle and the fact that a close associate of an apostle was not healed, shows that the dilemma has existed from the early days of the church. This should never discourage or introduce doubt to our prayers, but should serve as a guard against presumption or condemnation.

Sometimes God responds to our prayers of suffering by removing it. Other times He eases the suffering. Other times, He simply remains sufficient in our suffering. But make no mistake, He never abandons us in our suffering. He is with us in our garden of Gethsemane. Continue to pray, praise and seek Him. It is really the determining factor of whether we sink or swim. And remember, no matter what it looks like, we get to "get up" too!! If God doesn't heal us on earth, He will raise us up in His glorious presence. God did not save His own son from death, even though Jesus cried out. God had something much greater that would be accomplished.

When we have cried and prayed and fasted and, and, and—God does hear us whether He heals us or not. Keep trusting Him because something greater may be at stake. Something we may not know till we see Him.

Patiently waiting to see Him.

Who Do You Look Like?

What a day. It is one of my first days in awhile to get stuff planted and weeded and planted and weeded and of course, planted and weeded. It never ends, nor I doubt I would really want it to. Rick moved one of our cows to the neighbors lush pasture. I guess she had fear of being alone and jumped the fence. You know, I don't think I have ever seen a cow jump. As a kid, I guess I thought they jumped over the moon, but then fortunately I grew out of that. So for the afternoon, I chased a cow up and down the street and through the woods. Meanwhile, he walked right back through our neighbors gate which led into our pasture.

It could have been that simple, until the horses decided that the grass really is greener on the other side. Back to weeding. Dirt and animals are good for the soul, and honestly I don't know what I would have done over the last years without their antics to carry me through.

Onto more important topics! I came across a simple scripture that really should be my life verse. It was during the time when all hell broke loose in my life—I lost my two sons to tragedy and then my mother in less than a year. All I really prayed was, "Lord, show me how to look like You as I walk through this. This is way crazy, and I don't have a clue how to do it, but I want to!"

1 John 2:6 *He that saith he abideth in him ought himself also so to walk, even as he walked.*

I knew that I "knew" Jesus, so I simply looked at the scriptures to see how He walked through this crazy thing called life. Basically I saw that "he didn't walk by sight, but by faith in His Father" (2 Corinthians 5:7). He forgave, He didn't go to bed angry, He prayed, He taught, He healed, He cast out a few devils, He fried fish, and He walked! Okay, simple enough if you truly believe that you are one with Him.

Keep Walking..

Tandem jumps in skydiving is when you are strapped to the instructors back and jump together. That is kind of how I think we are supposed to do it with Jesus. Abide in Him (strap yourself to Him) and start walking (jumping). He will be right there guiding you through this thing called life, strapped on till you land!!

And lastly, two definitions that have helped me more than once.

Faith—God's Word is true.

Trust—even if things don't seem to be working, my position remains the same.

No matter what is looks like, God's promises are true, even if they are not apparent just quite yet.

Hebrews 6:12 *That ye be not slothful, but followers of them who through faith and patience inherit the promises.*

2 Corinthians 1:20 *For all the promises of God in him are yea, and in him Amen, unto the glory of God by us.*

Keep walking...

How's the Lifting?

Spring is a super busy time on the farm and I am about whooped! There is a lot of effort involved here, but the rewards are great. God's Word often reminds me of my farm job.

Psalm 121:1-8 *A Song of degrees. I will lift up mine eyes unto the hills, from whence cometh my help. My help cometh from the LORD, which made heaven and earth. He will not suffer thy foot to be moved: he that keepeth thee will not slumber. Behold, he that keepeth Israel shall neither slumber nor sleep. The LORD is thy keeper: the LORD is thy shade upon thy right hand. The sun shall not smite thee by day, nor the moon by night. The LORD shall preserve thee from all evil: he shall preserve thy soul. The LORD shall preserve thy going out and thy coming in from this time forth, and even for evermore.*

This Psalm really spoke to me this week. It is so nice that "I will lift and He helps!" In looking up the word "will" ("I will...") in the Hebrew it says "anything breathing." That's us!

When we "lift" we see that God never sleeps, He preserves us from all evil, and whether I am going in or out and forevermore, He preserves me. Now, that doesn't necessarily mean no adversity, but it does mean He brings us out to the other side. Look at the Hebrew boys who got dumped in the fire (Daniel 3). Fire either burns or purifies. It all depends if you are doing "fire" with or without Jesus. You decide!!

Keep lifting...

Keep Walking..

The Rock Foundation

I want to share some thoughts from "Biblical Incites to Food and Related Issues." This is a teaching that came out of years of eating disorders, Bachelor's and Master's degrees in Nutrition, and nine years studying and working in the natural medicine field. I am happy to report that God can do a lot with all of our striving and He graciously showed me what the Word had to say about food, nutrition, diets, etc. I promise you it was like nothing I ever learned in all my worldly knowledge!!

Colossians spells it out for us:

Colossians 2:16-17 *Let no man therefore judge you in meat, or in drink, or in respect of an holy day, or of the new moon, or of the sabbath days: Which are a shadow of things to come; but the body is of Christ.*

Colossians 2:20-23 *Wherefore if ye be dead with Christ from the rudiments of the world, why, as though living in the world, are ye subject to ordinances, (Touch not; taste not; handle not; Which all are to perish with the using;) after the commandments and doctrines of men? Which things have indeed a shew of wisdom in will worship, and humility, and neglecting of the body; not in any honour to the satisfying of the flesh.*

We spend so much time trying to follow legalistic ideas forced on us by the world and even religious leaders (and of course by the Dietitians - haha!!). That doesn't line up with the Word.

Wise leaders and servants should focus their lives on Jesus Christ and avoid presumptuous and transient teachings that may seem right at the time but don't hold water over time. I can't tell you how many different things about food and nutrition that have changed in my 31 years of being a Registered Dietitian. It used to be, for example, that coconut oil, butter, chocolate and coffee were bad for you. Now they are promoted as health-giving. And that transient list goes on and on!!

The Word is the only foundation for life that NEVER changes and can be easily "stood on" without falling off into space. Reject rules that aim to cleanse the spirit by means of humanly contrived regulations. Realize that in Christ you are no longer subject to human wisdom or works, but to God alone. It sure makes all your reading and decisions for life pretty simple... just stick with the Word that never changes because it doesn't need to. That's TRUTH and a time-saving tip for life!!

Stand on The Rock.

OCD or Grace?

Luke 5:36 *And he spake also a parable unto them; No man putteth a piece of a new garment upon an old; if otherwise, then both the new maketh a rent, and the piece that was taken out of the new agreeth not with the old.*

Once again, I want to focus on the difference between the old covenant, the law, and the new covenant which is of grace. The above scripture sums it up well and the word "agreeth" really brings it home. The verse is talking about the foolishness of taking the old covenant and trying to mix it with the new. If there is anything I have learned this year, it is the fact that the law and grace do not mix and never will. Moreover, it hinders our victorious walk as Christians and emits confusion to those who are watching our journey.

The word "agreeth" in the Greek means **sumphóneó**, which comes from our word symphony. Listening to a symphony, you hope that everyone is in harmony and playing their instruments together to create a most beautiful sound. If we apply the words that Jesus spoke in Luke 5:36, He is saying that when you try to mix the law with grace, it comes out like a symphony you wish you had never heard. No wonder people avoid Christianity when we operate out of mixture.

My prayer is that we will all examine ourselves and see where we are still trying to follow the "do's and don'ts" of the law. We need to see where we are jumping into a self-effort mode to get ourselves more spiritual and, as a result, are playing our own instruments all by ourselves (i.e., bad symphony!)

I recently heard this described as "OCD" or obsessive Christian disorder! God knew we couldn't live a perfect life and sent Jesus to forgive us of past, present and future sins.

Keep Walking...

In other words, we can never mess up if we are in Him. Wow, what a burden lifter! This makes me love Him even more; and isn't' that the goal after all?

Avoid mixture...

Keep Drinking

I sit here in beautiful Colorado feeling the effects of the altitude. The basic cure is more water, as it is in our walk with the Lord. The higher we go with Him, the more "watering" we need to grow. As I mentioned in a previous newsletter, our pastor states that when the Bible references "still" water, it is referring to God, and when it talks about moving water, it is referencing the Holy Spirit. Water is always good!!

Isaiah 44:3 *For I will pour water on him who is thirsty, And floods on the dry land; I will pour My Spirit on your descendants and My blessing on your offspring.*

If you are thirsty for more of God, He will pour out the Holy Spirit (moving water) on us and our families. I certainly pray that, right now, as we spend time with our grandchildren. I have to believe that He poured His Spirit out on my deceased children because I have been thirsty for quite awhile. His Word is true no matter what it looks like.

John 7:37-38 *On the last day, that great day of the feast, Jesus stood and cried out, saying, "If anyone thirsts, let him come to Me and drink. He who believes in Me, as the Scripture has said, out of his heart will flow rivers of living water."*

We fill up with Him and then He flows out of us. Those who are satisfied by Jesus will themselves become channels of spiritual refreshment for others. I continue to be so thirsty and need a lot of water for this altitude, physically and spiritually.

Water is always the answer.

Keep drinking.

Keep Walking...

Can You Really Believe God?

I am studying the book of John and am never ceased to be amazed at the simplicity of the Gospel, and that simplicity is to believe in Him. The Word is full of promises and so often we give it a quick glance, and if it doesn't "perform" we quickly give up on God and go to the next thing that might work. The word "believe" seems to be jumping out over and over in my study time and conversations with others.

In the first few chapters of the book of John, we find Jesus telling the servants to put water in the pots, we find the nobleman going home to his dying son and we find the very sick man by the pool of Bethesda. In all of this, when the people did what Jesus said and walked in belief, things happened. The water was turned to wine, the nobleman went home and found his son alive and the man in Bethesda picked up his bed and walked. These people did what Jesus told them with no questions, with full hearts of belief, and not needing to see signs and wonders first.

John 4:48-50 *Then said Jesus unto him, Except ye see signs and wonders, ye will not believe. The nobleman saith unto him, Sir, come down ere my child die. Jesus saith unto him, Go thy way; thy son liveth. And the man believed the word that Jesus had spoken unto him, and he went his way.*

That is a great thing, especially when it works so quickly. But what happens when you feel like you are trusting God, doing what you are asked, trying to walk in belief, and fighting off doubt?

You do what the Lord has shown me over and over; you keep walking and keep believing, knowing that it will come to pass.

Keep Walking..

There are several scriptures that jerk my chain in some fashion so that I want to shake my fist at God. But then, I must keep believing and knowing that truth is truth and God's promises are always yes.

Deuteronomy 30:19 *I call heaven and earth to record this day against you, that I have set before you life and death, blessing and cursing: therefore choose life, that both thou and thy seed may live:*

Mark 11:24 *Therefore I say unto you, What things soever ye desire, when ye pray, believe that ye receive them, and ye shall have them.*

Those scriptures really got my goat after I lost my sons, mom and sister. I had chosen life and blessings and it didn't seem like my seed "lived" at all. I prayed and believed and quoted "help my unbelief" but sickness or devastation did not go away.

"What's with that?" I asked God. God never said life, and health and fullness would be accomplished when I asked, but He promised it would. I thus have to believe that my water will turn to fine wine, that my sons will live and that if I pick up my bed, then I will keep walking and find that life will perform in abundance. To do this, I have to stretch my definition of life. I do not believe it is confined to these 70 plus years on earth which is where we often camp.

Mark says pray and "ye shall have them." That is a future tense statement that says in the Greek "it will come to pass!" It is life and if you are in Jesus, then that is eternal.

People often ask how I keep going and the answer is simply this: I am walking and believing that God will do what He said. Remember, He said "patiently" wait. Again, I find that when I do what He says, life is ever so much better. If He says to patiently wait, then I'll study and find that the word "patiently" in the Greek language, means cheerful endurance. If He says to "rejoice" in the midst of fiery trials **(1 Peter 4:12-13)**, then I'll muster up a praise to the Creator who has a creative solution for my life issues. If He says that His will is giving thanks in (not for) all things, then I better be thankful.

1 Thessalonians 5:18 *In every thing give thanks: for this is the will of God in Christ Jesus concerning you.*

As a new favorite song says, "If I'm gonna praise Him, gimme some room." Might as well "live it up!"

Get some room...

NUMB IS DUMB

I received a message today from a woman who is a house parent to troubled teenage boys asking me about my life experiences with marijuana. And yes, I have had them. Several of the boys admitted that they had been smoking pot when they would go to their homes on the weekend. She asked me (with all of my experience) what she could say that might make an impact. It was a hard question as marijuana had kept me numb enough to survive life. Nothing mattered so much when you were high; difficult situations were made easier because the "edges" had been dulled to a tolerable level. To be honest, I really felt like it was a medicine for depression that was "natural." Psychiatric medications were an unwelcomed alternative, and if you have ever taken some of them, I am sure you can relate. Many of them have horrible side effects.

Now I am sure these boys do not know the Bible well, but they can probably quote the verse about God making all herbs for man's use. I speak that from experience.

Genesis 1:29 *And God said, Behold, I have given you every herb bearing seed, which is upon the face of all the earth, and every tree, in the which is the fruit of a tree yielding seed; to you it shall be for meat.*

This is a perfect example of how we can make the scriptures work for us. We take them out of context. Nowhere does it say to grow something that is against the law, chop it up and roll it up in paper or stick it in two-foot pipes and smoke it! To be honest, if it weren't illegal by the laws of the land, I believe we could take it and sprinkle 1/2 teaspoon in spaghetti and be fine. We do that with other herbs and I am sure some of them make us feel better, even if just through our taste buds.

Keep Walking...

But the fact is the scriptures tell us we have to obey the law.

So what was I to say to the question that was being posed to me? If we look to Hosea and Proverbs, the answer shows itself (and it doesn't' have to just be about marijuana)!

Hosea 8:7 (NKJV) *They sow the wind, And reap the whirlwind: The stalk has no bud; It shall never produce meal. If it should produce, aliens would swallow it up.*

That pretty much sums up my marijuana days. I had planted nothing of value, but rather a numbing avoidance of God and false ability that I could take care of my own needs. Yes, I "grew" a stalk but it didn't produce any fruit in my life or for other people. Of course at that time in my life (and sometimes now-ugh) I am interested in myself only. It never dawned on me to try to be producing something for someone else. Life was simply a survival operation. I imagine that is what these boys are dealing with in their lives. If we could just get them, and us, to understand sowing and reaping; but it's hard when you are just trying to keep your land (life) from going to foreclosure. There is not much energy for tilling and digging and preparing a soil for good seed.

Proverbs 22:8 *He that soweth iniquity shall reap vanity: and the rod of his anger shall fail.*

Oh, if we could all see, that when we sow things that are not of God, we reap "nothingness." I think our anger and self works (i.e. handling things ourselves) is one of the main causes of sin and they both fail in getting the results we are really after. It ends up being a lot of energy spent for nothing. I doubt that is ever our goal.

The Bible says our born again life is a mystery and is disclosed only to those who believe. I can only pray for salvation and open my heart to receive the life, death and resurrection of Jesus.

Keep Walking..

"God open our eyes and let us make a clear decision of exactly what we truly want in life. We want full vibrant relationships, provision, peace, joy and good times. We can only understand those if we understand that You are those desires. Help us to seek You, and through You, begin to plant these things in our lives. Then and only then, can we truly give up the numbing things of this world. And while we are at it, we pray for a bumper crop!!"

Feeling life...

Keep Walking...

God's Working Ears

I would like to look at John 11:41-42 for a simple but succinct prayer.

John 11:41-42 *Then they took away the stone from the place where the dead was laid. And Jesus lifted up his eyes, and said, Father, I thank thee that thou hast heard me. And I knew that thou hearest me always: but because of the people which stand by I said it, that they may believe that thou hast sent me.*

What if every time we prayed, the first words out of our mouth were, "Father, I thank you that you have heard me." The word "heard" is past tense, and that is what makes all the difference in the world. These words are a great confidence in the true power of God, and are a reassurance to us that He does hear and answer our prayers. Somehow, saying it at the beginning of every prayer emphasizes that "His eye is on the sparrow," He knows every detail before it happens, and He is in total control.

In vs. 42, Jesus shows us His confidence in His prayer to raise Lazarus from the dead and that God hears us, and wants us to be confident as well. So often we pray... and pray... and pray because it is the right thing to do. The problem is we keep praying as if to remind God and ourselves of what is needed. What if we could really BELIEVE the fact that when we pray, God actually HEARS us the first time.

I remember praying everyday for my son Dustin who had been in a horrible car accident. I prayed for every part of his body, every neuron, and every cell to be as God intended from the foundation of the earth. One day as I was praying and walking, which is my everyday habit, God said," I heard you the first time." In a nutshell, I was praying out of fear. It was as if I didn't pray, his

Keep Walking..

health would go downhill. God loves our prayers but He would prefer a "thank you Father that you have heard me" prayer versus a fear-based prayer that is based on US praying and hoping we don't forget something.

My prayers continued, but my attitude towards them changed. I would start out saying, "Thank you Father that you have heard my prayer." From there, it was an emphasis on the fact that God was already in action bringing forth HIS best plan and I needed to let my control go. I was BELIEVING He heard me.

I must admit that I don't always like God's answers, but I have learned to trust Him, that He knows best for bringing His plan and glory to the earth. Most of you know that Dustin died almost one year after his accident. I remember being upset with God and reminding Him that He didn't answer one prayer of mine. He quickly showed me that He answered every one, just not in the way that I thought He should.

I had prayed for Dustin's salvation and in the hospital was able to lead him to the Lord while on a ventilator and full of pain medication. He was able to form every word and look me in the eye as we prayed. That was a priceless answer to a prayer. My other zillion prayers for healing were heard as well, and yes Dustin is perfectly healed—just not on earth. Every body part, every neuron, and every cell is totally healed.

God—You did hear my prayers and You did raise him from the dead. He was lost but now he is found... right up there with You. So Dustin, and Forrest and all my other family members who are "alive without their bodies"— see ya later.

Heaven on Earth...

Keep Walking...

Unity Equals Power

Most of you know of my heart for community, and a weekly community Bible study at the local library seemed to fit the bill. I can't think of anything I would like better than for all races and all denominations to come together in unity. That is when the Church will find the fullness of its power. It seems like we have a long way to go, but I do not give up hope.

Acts 2:1-2 *And when the day of Pentecost was fully come, they were all with one accord in one place. And suddenly there came a sound from heaven as of a rushing mighty wind, and it filled all the house where they were sitting.*

Acts 2:4 *And they were all filled with the Holy Ghost, and began to speak with other tongues, as the Spirit gave them utterance.*

I recently counted all the "they's" found in the book of Acts. To my closest count, there are 164 "they's" in the book of Acts, alone! All the power of the early church came from them all working on the same page. I challenge you to read the book of Acts and see how the early church was of "one accord" and how great things happened. That is why the enemy works so hard at getting things divided. Whether it is a husband and wife, a family, a church, a business, a country or any number of things, He knows division causes defeat. We see in the Old Testament when "they" were building the Tower of Babel (not good in God's eyes) and God's response was:

Genesis 11:6 *And the LORD said, Behold, the people is one, and they have all one language; and this they begin to do: and now nothing will be restrained from them, which they have imagined to do.*

He knew that if He didn't divide them they would build this big idol. He knew that unity equals power and that is what He wants in the church—a body of believers—that are all on the same page, His page! He is then able to use each of us and pour out all of His gifts for the good of all.

Ephesians 4:2-6 *With all lowliness and meekness, with longsuffering, forbearing one another in love; Endeavouring to keep the unity of the Spirit in the bond of peace. There is one body, and one Spirit, even as ye are called in one hope of your calling; One Lord, one faith, one baptism, One God and Father of all, who is above all, and through all, and in you all.*

Ephesians 4:13 *Till we all come in the unity of the faith, and of the knowledge of the Son of God, unto a perfect man, unto the measure of the stature of the fulness of Christ:*

Ephesians 4:16 *From whom the whole body fitly joined together and compacted by that which every joint supplieth, according to the effectual working in the measure of every part, maketh increase of the body unto the edifying of itself in love.*

And this is what is might just look like!! (Video—Hezekiah Walker—"Every Praise")

Keep the unity!

Keep Walking...

BE A GOOD SMELL

I have a simple question for you: Do you know that believers and the gospel have a smell? We should know this. Here is what the word says about it:

2 Corinthians 2:14-16 *Now thanks be unto God, which always leads us in triumph in Christ and through us diffuses the fragrance of His knowledge in every place. For we are to God the fragrance of Christ among those who are being saved and among those who are perishing. To the one, we are the aroma of death leading to death; and to the other the aroma of life leading to life. And who is sufficient for these things?*

I love how Paul is talking about "in Christ," and through us the "smell" of the gospel is diffused. The fragrance of the knowledge of Christ is simply the gospel. Those who reject the gospel, smell death. Those who are being saved find the knowledge of Christ to be an aroma of life leading to life which is the Good News.

Philippians 4:18 *But I have all, and abound: I am full, having received of Epaphroditus the things which were sent from you, an odour of a sweet smell, a sacrifice acceptable, wellpleasing to God.*

In this passage, we have the Philippians who have made sacrifices to provide for Paul, which he describes as a sweet smell and fully agreeable to God. When we are generous, we "smell" good and God receives it. Lastly, we see our prayers have a smell. God inhales the prayers of the saints.

Revelation 5:8 *And when he had taken the book, the four beasts and four and twenty elders fell down before the Lamb, having every one of them harps, and golden vials full of odours, which are the prayers of saints.*

In summary, we see the sweet smell of the gospel by generously helping and serving others, and our prayers as sweet sacrifices that make God "notice" us. I think we can see that as well, in our surroundings when we get around a child of God. There is something about them, perhaps a sweet smelling sacrifice, that we notice. It's just a really nice and pleasurable feeling. It makes me happy to think that perhaps when I am "smelling good for God" that He too is having a nice and pleasurable experience smelling me!!

Keep diffusing a good smell!

Why, Why, Why?

The summer seems like it is in a very fast-paced march. I guess, in a sense, that is beneficial because the devil knows his time is short and we are marching fast to that fulfillment. It seems to me that the devil has a vacuum cleaner way of life and communication that can easily suck the life right out of us without us even being aware.

I remember when I used the shop vac for the first time and saw that if you didn't put the hose on the right side, you could get blown away. We need to put our vacuum cleaners on the side that "blows away" when dealing with the defeat, depression and hopelessness that the devil tries to attack us with. HE is dirt and we can blow him away with the power of the Living God in us.

Romans 8:11 *But if the Spirit of him that raised up Jesus from the dead dwell in you, he that raised up Christ from the dead shall also quicken your mortal bodies by his Spirit that dwelleth in you.*

So now that you can be assured of the power in you, how can you manifest this in real life and real situations? Talk to yourself, talk to yourself, talk to yourself (with scripture)! When the Bible says something once, we know it is Truth and good for us to understand. When it is said twice, take notice. But when it says it three times, exactly the same, you best get it deep into your spirit man because you are going to need it, and God knows that!

Psalm 42:5 *Why art thou cast down, O my soul? and why art thou disquieted in me? hope thou in God: for I shall yet praise him for the help of his countenance.*

Psalm 42:11 *Why art thou cast down, O my soul? and why art thou disquieted within me? hope thou in God: for I*

Keep Walking..

shall yet praise him, who is the health of my countenance, and my God.

Psalm 43:5 *Why art thou cast down, O my soul? and why art thou disquieted within me? hope in God: for I shall yet praise him, who is the health of my countenance, and my God.*

When I am getting sucked up like too much dirt on the floor on the high setting, I better start talking to myself. It goes something like this:

"Why am I getting so down (or worried, or hopeless, or defeated, or, or, or), and why am I allowing this loud sound raging (Hebrew for "disquieted) in me? I am instructed by my awesome Father to wait, be patient and trust (hope). I think I'll just praise Him who is the salvation (Hebrew— saved, delivered, victory, prosperity, and health—wow!) of my face- the part that turns (countenance) God!"

I love the Hebrew word for countenance. It means "face —the part that turns." Questioning myself as to why I am down and why am I allowing this loud noise of heaviness and then trusting in God and praising Him, turns me around and turns the devil around to flee. Blow him away with the other side of the shop-vac with the triple Word that God has spoken. As we used to say in 12 step programs—"it works if you work it."

Keep blowing...

Keep Walking...

Praise, Trust and Delivered

I hope everyone is preparing for celebrating our freedom in this country. Please remember that freedom is not free. There is a huge cost and the cost is found in many areas. Jesus also paid the ultimate price for our freedom. We can't pay for that freedom, all we can do is humbly accept it as a gift. It is so hard for us to accept gifts, as we have been trained that we have to "do" something for it or pay it back in some way. That is probably why it is so hard for us to fully accept salvation. We don't know how to just receive and then the battle begins. We either try to do something or we just reject the gift partially or altogether, so we don't have to deal with it.

Most of us have accepted what our soldiers have done for our freedom, at a great price, and are very grateful. Why do we struggle so hard to receive what Jesus is offering: His grace, His forgiveness of past, present and future sins, and His righteousness? The new covenant is about us receiving, period. The old covenant was that God would bless us if we followed the law and curse us if we failed. In His mercy and love, He saw that, knowing that it wouldn't work. All along He was showing us we would need a Savior.

The new covenant is so easy; it humbles us to our knees which we don't really like. God says that He'll send Jesus to fully deliver us and provide for our righteousness and all we have to do is receive. We squirm, we run the other way, we work, work, work, and then we try to justify it all to be a "good Christian." Maybe we just need to say thank you and spend our efforts on praising Him.

Psalm 22:3-5 *But thou art holy, O thou that inhabitest the praises of Israel. Our fathers trusted in thee: they trusted, and thou didst deliver them. They cried unto thee, and were delivered: they trusted in thee, and were not confounded.*

Keep Walking..

The key words here are "praise, trusted and delivered." Could salvation really be that simple? Can we simply receive our salvation, praise Him for it, trust in Him and be delivered. Probably so, if we would believe and walk in it. Don't try to buy or pay back that freedom that has been freely given. Simply receive it and share it with others.

I often think about our soldiers returning from Vietnam. They didn't expect people to "pay" them, but only to receive them and for what they fought so diligently for. Instead we spit on them, rejected them and turned them away. I wonder if that is how Jesus feels when we don't humbly receive what He did. There is something that I always try to do when I meet a soldier that fought in Vietnam and that is to tell him, "welcome home." Maybe, just maybe, we need to tell Jesus, "welcome home, come dwell in my temple freely." That's all He ever asked anyway. Think about it and then get on with your "freedom celebration" this week.

Be free...

One Nation Under God

A wet and soggy, happy July 4th to you all as we commemorate the adoption of the Declaration of Independence on July 4, 1776, declaring independence from the kingdom of Great Britain.

If we relate that to biblical terms, it is like us declaring our deliverance and walking out in freedom from a stronghold that has held us in its clutches. However, if you watch the news, it seems that we are selling out our freedom at a very high cost. The hard thing to hear and watch is the passivity and blindness that is occurring. The government choices all seem to be a good idea to our elected officials who represent us, while many of us raise our hands and hearts in horror. Watching all of this can bring much fear unless we turn back to the simple, but all powerful words of God.

Proverbs 21:1 *The king's heart is in the hand of the LORD, as the rivers of water: he turneth it whithersoever he will.*

God is allowing all of this to happen just as He did in the Old Testament. The Israelites would turn away from God and start sacrificing to idols and He would send the evil kings to take them captive and back into slavery or destruction. They would finally get it and cry out to God. Of course, He would hear their prayer and deliver them until the next time. It would then happen all over again. My notes in the book of Lamentations state that the people knew that it was God (rather than man) that had allowed their situation. God did this, not in hatred, but in a desire that their suffering would direct them back towards Him. That is His jealousy for us and relentless love to have us return into relationship with Him. He will pursue us to the end.

Okay, back to the original concept. We need not fear what is going on or be distraught that this nation is go-

Keep Walking..

ing to hell in a hand basket. As a nation, we have turned from God and if He can have His way, as the suffering begins, we will turn back to Him. It's His way. Personally I believe that we must all continue to pray and trust that it is only God that can turn the heart of our nation back to Him...*as the rivers of water!*

Psalm 37:1 *A Psalm of David. Fret not thyself because of evildoers, neither be thou envious against the workers of iniquity.*

Psalm 37:7-8 *Rest in the LORD, and wait patiently for him: fret not thyself because of him who prospereth in his way, because of the man who bringeth wicked devices to pass. Cease from anger, and forsake wrath: fret not thyself in any wise to do evil.*

God said "fret not" three times in this one Psalm. As I was thinking about today's topic, the "fret not" Psalm came to mind. I sat down, as I do every day, and God confirmed the message. The July 4, Oswald Chambers daily devotion was about "fret not." Let me share the direct words of Mr. Chambers:

"It is one thing to say "Do not fret" but something very different to have such a nature that you find yourself unable to fret. It's easy to say "rest in the Lord and wait patiently for Him" (vs. 7) until our own little world is turned upside down and we are forced to live in confusion and agony like so many other people... If this "Do not" doesn't work there, then it will not work anywhere. This "Do not" must work during our days of difficulty and uncertainty, as well as our peaceful days or it will never work. Resting in the Lord is not dependent on your external circumstance at all, but on your relationship with God Himself... Fretting rises from our determination to have our own way."

Our nation is in a sad state, but God is still in charge. He tells us that He is the one that turns the heart of the King and reminds us to fret not. Are you going to trust Him or not?

Keep Walking...

On this day of independence, allow God to deliver you from the stronghold of anxiety and worry.

Luke 12:32 *Fear not, little flock; for it is your Father's good pleasure to give you the kingdom.*

No fretting!

Keep Stepping

Do you ever wonder about the steps you take each day that unfold as your life?

Psalm 37:23-24 *The steps of a good man are ordered by the LORD: and he delighteth in his way. Though he fall, he shall not be utterly cast down: for the LORD upholdeth him with his hand.*

Do you often chastise yourself for some of your decisions as a believer, or think you should have figured it out a little better? This verse really showed me that if I have a heart for God, even if it isn't always outwardly showing, that He still has my back and is leading me. My steps are ordered by God and He is delighted in the path and work that will hopefully transform me to be more like Him. He likes my crazy path, that I think I am messing up on a daily basis!!! That excites me and frees me from having to do it all right!

The Word goes on to say that if I fall, it is not the end of the world because He is holding me in His hand. If we could just really get a physical, mental and spiritual picture of God holding us in His hand, I think we might be able to rest a bit from all of our striving. He already knows we fall and has that mighty Right Hand stretched out waiting. I love the second half of this Proverb:

Proverbs 11:9 *An hypocrite with his mouth destroyeth his neighbour: but through knowledge shall the just be delivered.*

If I can only captivate the knowledge that God is ordering my steps, then I might just get delivered from things that "dog" me on a regular basis. To summarize, my "bread" for the day, I can rest assured and know that every step I take is hand-picked by God for my best journey. If I have a little crash on the way, it is okay

Keep Walking...

because His loving hand upholds me off the hard, black, hot asphalt of destruction. The following is a favorite scripture that I pray regularly. I think it relates well:

Psalm 119:133 *Order my steps in thy word: and let not any iniquity have dominion over me.*

And then a bonus while looking for verse 133:

Psalm 119:117 *Hold thou me up, and I shall be safe: and I will have respect unto thy statutes continually.*

Hebrews 3:14...*steadfast unto the end.*

Keep stepping...

More Saved, More Healed, More Righteous?

Do you ever try new religious methods hoping to get something more spiritual accomplished?

Luke 11:24-26 *When the unclean spirit is gone out of a man, he walketh through dry places, seeking rest; and finding none, he saith, I will return unto my house whence I came out. And when he cometh, he findeth it swept and garnished. Then goeth he, and taketh to him seven other spirits more wicked than himself; and they enter in, and dwell there: and the last state of that man is worse than the first.*

These are the Words of Jesus and He is using this parable to show how Israel was, in worse state than before He came to give her light. Of course, it is also showing that the state of a backslider is worse after being saved and going back into sin. The real issue, however, is those who lack the spiritual discernment to recognize Jesus as the Savior. In rejecting Him, Israel had nothing left but empty rites and ceremonies making them even more susceptible to Satan's deception. We are no different.

So often we get saved and then launch into various methods of getting "more saved," "more healed," "more righteous," and in doing this, we kind of forget Jesus!! This may lead us into some biblical methods, but again, we lose our focus on Christ crucified. It is ONLY because of the death, burial and resurrection of Jesus, that righteousness, healing, deliverance, etc., are even remote possibilities. We seek healing versus the healer. In reality, we are seeking something fleshly instead of a spiritual relationship with Jesus. Think about it. I want my achy, diseased flesh to get better. That is a part of salvation, but I think God is more interested in spiritual healing than healing of our flesh. We are very familiar with this scripture:

Isaiah 53:5 *But he was wounded for our transgressions, he was bruised for our iniquities: the chastisement of our peace was upon him; and with his stripes we are healed.*

The Hebrew word for stripes means "bruise, wound," but it also comes from a root word (H2266) meaning "to join, and to have fellowship with." So if we put that in today's language, it might go something like this: "By joining and having fellowship with Jesus Christ, I am already healed."

It is one thing to cast out an unclean spirit and quite another thing to have a deep, passionate, intimate relationship with Jesus. Great relationships never involve empty rites and ceremonies. They rely on a covenant walk through great times and tough times. The "times" don't really matter, it is Who you are privileged to have walking with you through it all. That really matters!

Righteous, saved, healed, and delivered—period!

Prison Boldness

We are marching into March, another form of "keep walking." If you have ever felt discouraged in your walk with the Lord, or felt condemned because of your situation, then you might want to pay attention to the following scriptures. Here we have the author of much of the New Testament, Paul, in prison, not at all worried about what others are thinking of him as a prominent Christian in dire straits.

Philippians 1:12 *But I would ye should understand, brethren, things that happened unto me have fallen out rather unto the furtherance of the gospel; So that my bonds in Christ are manifest in all the palace, and in all other places;*

Actually, Paul is pretty pumped up about being in prison because he gets to share the Good News to all of the elite Roman palace guards and the other prisoners. I mean what are they going to do, lock him up?? Because of his boldness to share, we see that it rubbed off on others and they began to share as well. It was infectious.

Philippians 1:15 *Some indeed preach Christ even of envy and strife; and some also of good will:*

Some were preaching out of the abundance of their heart, while others were mocking Paul out of jealousy. Paul didn't really care either way, he was just thrilled that the word of God was being spoken!

Philippians 1:18 *What then? notwithstanding, every way, whether in pretence, or in truth, Christ is preached; and I therein do rejoice, yea, and will rejoice.*

Lastly, Paul is not one bit concerned about where he is in his Christian walk, about his "thorn," about his surroundings, or about how he got there. He is only

Keep Walking...

concerned about one thing, and that is representing Jesus in the midst of life... or death.

Philippians 1:20 *According to my earnest expectation and my hope, that in nothing I shall be ashamed, but that with all boldness, as always, so now also Christ shall be magnified in my body, whether it be by life, or by death.*

Let people see your faith in the midst of the battle. There is no victory without a battle. If we kind of pull out when things are going tough so no one will "see us," our strong faith can't be seen. If our faith can't be seen, then Christianity is just another thing to pull out to show off when things are prospering.

1 Thessalonians 1:8 *For from you sounded out the word of the Lord not only in Macedonia and Achaia, but also in every place your faith to God-ward is spread abroad; so that we need not to speak anything.*

The Thessalonians' faith showed so much, not a word was needed. It was real, demonstrated and alive!

Let your faith be seen, as you wait for Jesus, no matter what the situation you find yourself in.

Keep marching...

SEEDS

I am stuck on spring-time stuff, so today I wanted to talk about seeds. There are so many scriptures in the New and Old Testament that use the word "seed," and in many different contexts. Sometimes it hurts because many of the scriptures seem to be talking about our "seed" and mine aren't here. Often, I want to hurry through these passages and get it over with.

As I studied the concordance, the general definition of seed is "the essential element of transmitting life." Seed is descriptive of course of our ancestry, it is also figurative of true believers (Romans 9:7,8,29; 1 Peter 1:23; Galatians 3:29) and of sowing God's Word (Matthew 13); Spiritual blessings (1 Corinthians 9:11), Christ's death (John 12:24) and the Christian's body (1 Corinthians 15:36-49).

The use of the word seed in the Old Testament (Hebrew), used 202 times, always has the same definitions which is "seed, fruit, plant, sowing time." In the New Testament, it is used 52 times and the Greek definition means "something sown, a remnant; offspring."

I am encouraged by these meanings. There are so many ways to sow seed to "transmit life." I can scatter smiles, spend time with you, study the Word with others, cook a meal and a gazillion other things to bring life. It is good to have children, but when life happens, or doesn't for that matter, we must always remember that we all have seed to transmit life to others.

So put on those muck boots sitting beside the door and get on out and sow. It is springtime ya know!! And when winter comes, keep sowing, it will bring forth much fruit when it warms up. We are not in charge of the seasons but we are in charge of farming.

Matthew 13:23 *But he that received seed into the good ground is he that heareth the word, and understands it; which also beareth fruit, and bringeth forth, some an hundredfold, some sixty, some thirty.*

Keep farming.

Keep Walking..

Quiet Yourself

I wanted to share a very simple Psalm with a very powerful message. I recently posted a picture on Facebook of a group of children, all with artificial legs, with smiles on their faces, getting ready to run a race. My somewhat snide comment was, "Take note crabby people and get over yourself!" Maybe I shouldn't have said that, but let's look at what God says!

Psalm 131:1-3 *¹LORD, my heart is not haughty, nor mine eyes lofty: neither do I exercise myself in great matters, or in things too high for me. ²Surely I have behaved and quieted myself, as a child that is weaned of his mother: my soul is even as a weaned child. ³Let Israel hope in the LORD from henceforth and forever.*

Let me throw in a few Hebrew words and call it a good day with a good message:

- Verse 1 - LORD, my feelings, will and intellect are not proud, nor my countenance, outward appearance, or that which flows from me, actively high; neither do I walk myself in matters too great or difficult for me.

- Verse 2 - Surely, I have calmed myself and taken my peace as a child that is treated well of his mother—my very needy (I added that!) person who is no longer dependent on others.

What I hear the voice of the LORD saying is to trust Him, i.e., don't, through your own efforts get into things that are over your head. Let Him guide you into the things that HE has given the abilities and grace to accomplish for Him. Each day we need to seek Him, instead of acting like whiny babies demanding others to take care of us. We need to learn to quiet OURSELVES in God, and not depend on others to hand us the pacifier we think we need.

Keep Walking...

And one more scripture:

Psalm 61:2 *From the end of the earth will I cry unto thee, when my heart is overwhelmed: lead me to the rock that is higher than I.*

Quiet yourself in God...

Keep Walking..

HE, HE, HE

We traveled to Virginia to celebrate my nephew's graduation from college. My deceased sister would have been very proud, I just wished she could have been there.

Vacations and traveling always conjures up visions of not having to work. Let these scriptures settle into your heart and go on "vacation" forever!!

Psalm 138:8 *The LORD will perfect that which concerneth me: thy mercy, O LORD, endureth for ever: forsake not the works of thine own hands.*

I love this because God is doing the perfecting and bringing to completion all that He has planned for me. The work "perfect" in the Hebrew language means to "end or finish; to cease to perform." God begins to work out His purposes in our lives, and continues His work until it is absolutely and completely done. Every molecule, every miscarried infant, every person in our life that dies prematurely, has been a perfect completed work of God's own hands. Where in the world did I get the idea that self effort would perfect me? Certainly not the Bible!! Here "He" goes again, performing the good work in us!

Philippians 1:6 *Being confident of this very thing, that he which hath begun a good work in you will perform it until the day of Jesus Christ:*

And one more time, it is the God of all grace that will make me perfect, strengthened and settled:

1 Peter 5:10 *But the God of all grace, who hath called us unto his eternal glory by Christ Jesus, after that ye have suffered a while, make you perfect, stablish, strengthen, settle you.*

Keep Walking...

It is He, He, He, He that makes, leads and restores!

Psalm 23:2-3 *He maketh me to lie down in green pastures: He leadeth me beside the still waters. He restoreth my soul: he leadeth me in the paths of righteousness for his name's sake.*

Keep He, He, He (ing).

The Broken Road is Blessed

I missed each of you on the conference call last week. I was out hiking and spending time with my nephews. The time to bond with my sister's children was priceless and I pray we planted at least a seed or two.

This past week, I seemed to be struggling over relationship issues and lost dreams. When I turned to God, (because really where else is there to turn that never fails), I quickly realized that our thought patterns are usually all twisted up. As I listened to the song entitled, "God Bless the Broken Road," by Selah, the words sang volumes to me. It talks about those who bring brokenness, hurt or oppression to us are really "Northern Stars leading us to Him."

He can also use long-lost dreams if I can venture to lay down my own and trust Him. Instead of being so frustrated with life, I was able to hear how "life" really is a great asset to me if I allow it. I am certainly considering it, knowing that God has a perfect story for my life. I do feel that the road I have walked has been a bit broken, but as the song says, "God blesses the broken road which leads straight to Him." I was getting a little bit oppressed and sad as I heard so many prayer needs, situations that seem impossible and things that bring hopelessness. But then I know, because I know, that God can do a great work in the midst of the most fiery trials.

So often we pray to draw closer to God and His response is to send "Northern Stars" to help us. I call it horrifically wonderful... horrific because of what we must go through, wonderful because we see the true nature of the grace of God in our lives and hopefully spiritual growth. Don't fight the effort with your own strength, you will end up a whipped puppy. Instead embrace the opportunity to draw closer to the Loving God.

Keep Walking...

The Psalms and Jeremiah says the help of man is useless anyway. So why do we put so much stock in man's opinions? Let God's opinion matter most and hurts will melt away.

Psalm 60:11 *Give us help from trouble: for vain is the help of man.*

Psalm 146:3 *Put not your trust in princes, nor in the son of man, in whom there is no help.*

Jeremiah 17:5 *Thus saith the LORD; Cursed be the man that trusteth in man, and maketh flesh his arm, and whose heart departeth from the LORD.*

Of course we need one another, but when we depend on "one another" instead of God, He may have an "interesting" way of bringing us back to Him.

God bless YOUR broken road.

(Song – God Bless the Broken Road - Selah)

Quit Working

I am still stuck on the whole concept of the New Covenant in that the only part I have to do is to believe. It is so much easier, and the rewards seem so much more satisfying, when you try to do things yourself in much activity. We think we are pleasing God and filling up our "gold star" chart to get the big prize such as healing or a financial blessing or something else we are trying to work for from God.

John 6:27-28 *Labour not for the meat which perisheth, but for that meat which endureth unto everlasting life, which the Son of man shall give unto you: for him hath God the Father sealed. Then said they unto him, What shall we do, that we might work the works of God? Jesus answered and said unto them, This is the work of God, that ye believe on him whom he hath sent.*

We "labour" so hard to get God to heal our physical bodies or clean up our messes. Seeking God for healing and certainly praying in all situations is absolutely important, not necessarily to get what you want, but to get "Him" and deepen that relationship that never perishes but endures!

I love verse 28 where the people ask what work they needed to do to ultimately please God. The answer is so simple, but yet so hard. Jesus says that the work of God is to believe in Jesus.

Mark 5:36 *As soon as Jesus heard the word that was spoken, he saith unto the ruler of the synagogue, Be not afraid, only believe.*

Keep meditating on this "only believe;" you might just find that you are not working so hard, not so tired, fearful and stressed out. The bottom line- you might just be beginning to understand and receive the covenant of

Keep Walking...

Grace that has been so freely given to you if you will only believe!!

Romans 6:14 *For sin shall not have dominion over you: for ye are not under the law, but under grace.*

Ephesians 2:8 *For by grace are ye saved through faith; and that not of yourselves: it is the gift of God:*

Romans 11:6 *And if by grace, then is it no more of works: otherwise grace is no more grace. But if it be of works, then is it no more grace: otherwise work is no more work.*

I couldn't resist adding these three scriptures. The only reason we try to work so hard to please God is that we still think we are filthy sinners because we keep "breaking the rules" (i.e. -the Law). Read clearly above that sin shall not have dominion over you because you are not under the law, but under the grace of God that has forgiven ALL sin, past, present and future!! If we keep working to receive the covenant of grace, then "grace is no more grace." Go on vacation from your works and just believe!!

Quit working...

Turn, Turn, Turn

I faintly detect a little bit of coolness in the air. The season is changing, just as God said it always would. Sometimes we feel like things in our life are never going to change. God's Word says differently and, as always, you have to decide whose report you are going to believe. Many of us have heard the following scripture, if not from the Bible but from the old song by the Birds. I remember my son Dustin coming home from school one day saying they had "studied" that particular song. I wondered if it might just be a teacher trying to bring some Christianity into the school, since she mentioned that is was "originally" from the Bible. I had certainly hoped so. God's Saints have a great way of representing Him in subtle, but profound ways.

So here goes (and I never get tired of reading it!):

Ecclesiastes 3:1-8

[1] To everything there is a season, and a time to every purpose under the heaven. [2] A time to be born, and a time to die; a time to plant, and a time to pluck up that which is planted; [3] A time to kill, and a time to heal; a time to break down, and a time to build up; [4] A time to weep, and a time to laugh; a time to mourn, and a time to dance; [5] A time to cast away stones, and a time to gather stones together; a time to embrace, and a time to refrain from embracing; [6] A time to get, and a time to lose; a time to keep, and a time to cast away; [7] A time to rend, and a time to sew; a time to keep silence, and a time to speak; [8] A time to love, and a time to hate, a time of war, and a time of peace.

I think the thing that I love the most about this, and even about the calendar season, is that I know, that I know, that no matter what, winter comes, followed by spring, followed by summer, which then ushers in fall. There is nothing I or anyone else can do to stop it.

So it goes with situations in our life. We may be in a great situation, or facing a tragedy or disease or loss of a job or whatever, but that season will be followed by a spring of new life, summer heat perhaps to burn up the fluff, then the ushering in of an outpouring of color—crispness and relief from the heat. So goes life! Don't hate the season, embrace it knowing that it has its purpose.

Another scripture that has helped me in the darkest times also comes from Ecclesiastes, which happens to be one of my favorite books. It reminds me of how Solomon (and myself) tried really hard to do life without God and finally came to the great understanding that it never works. Sometimes that lesson can take a long time, but God is a jealous God and never gives up on us. No matter what you are going through, remember the words of the wisest man on earth:

Ecclesiastes 7:8 *Better is the end of a thing than the beginning thereof: and the patient in spirit is better than the proud in spirit.*

If the end is better than the beginning, we can walk through whatever our Sovereign God has designed and know that when we come out on the other side, it will be awesome. That certainly puts a huge dent on the fear and dread and hopelessness that plagues our thoughts. Instead it provides a boost of hope and confidence in our Faithful God!

This song follows the scripture almost word for word! Who would have thought this in the sixties?

Keep turning...

(Song- Turn, Turn, Turn -The Byrds)

Keep Walking..

Chronic Sympathy – the Great Destroyer

I was meditating on this message and I came across the scriptures that seemed to describe my thoughts. That then took me to a very favorite passage from the devotional book, "Our Utmost for His Highest," by Oswald Chambers. If you do not have this book, I highly recommend it. The insights he expresses of the Living Word have truly changed my life. As I began to read, I decided that I needed to type out the entire page and then follow with the scriptures the Lord has shown me on this topic. I guess I could also give this message the title, "No Rescuing." Maybe that sounds harsh, but not if you can accept that God does His greatest work through tough times.

When people used to confide to me that their troubled son or daughter was going to jail, I wanted to shout "Hallelujah." I have found that many people come to know the Lord in deep and powerful ways in a cell. Some of the greatest ministries go on in prisons. A prison with a great ministry sure can beat the streets of the world!

Okay—word for word, the devotional from Oswald Chambers on May 3.

Ephesians 6:18 *Praying always with all prayer and supplication in the Spirit.*

"As we continue on in our intercession for others, we may find that our obedience to God in interceding is going to cost those for whom we intercede more than we ever thought. The danger in this is that we begin to intercede in sympathy with those whom God was gradually lifting up to a totally different level in direct answer to our prayers. Whenever we step back from our close identification with God's interest and concern for others and step into having emotional sympathy with them, the vital connection with God is gone.

We have the put our sympathy and concern for them in the way, and this is a deliberate rebuke to God.

It is impossible for us to have living and vital intercession unless we are perfectly and completely sure of God. And the greatest destroyer of that confident relationship to God, so necessary for intercession, is our own personal sympathy and preconceived bias. Identification with God is the key to intercession, and whenever we stop being identified with Him it is because of our sympathy with others, not because of sin. It is not likely sin will interfere with our intercessory relationship with God, but sympathy will. It is sympathy with ourselves or with others that makes us say, "I will not allow that thing to happen." and instantly we are out of that vital connection with God.

Vital intercession leaves you with neither the time nor the inclination to pray for your own "sad and pitiful self." You do not have to struggle to keep thoughts of yourself out, because they are not even there to be kept out of your thinking. You are completely and entirely identified with God's interests and concerns in other lives. God gives us discernment in the lives of others to call us to intercession for them, never so that we may find fault with them."

Avoid operating out of sympathy which means "the sameness of feeling." If we could let go of our own fears about situations in our own lives and others, imagine the work God could do in answer to our prayers. I pray that you will seek God's perfect will for others and yourself, versus the plans that comfort and keep us comforted.

I promise God's plans, although extreme at times, will burn up the destructible and refine the indestructible. And that is true "beauty for ashes."

Keep practicing...

ALLOW THE FIRE

Our previous message was about "allowing" people to go through difficult times—believing that God was possibly doing His greatest work in the situation.

I also stated that we need to "avoid operating out of sympathy" in regards to another person. Please note the word is "operating," or continuing for a prolonged period of time, in sympathy. This "sameness or sharing of feelings" can bring on co-dependency. Satan begins to move in and to steal your identity in Christ. Your identity in Christ can assist someone in moving forward through the trial instead of getting stuck in the situation with the person because of your own fears.

What does the Word say about co-dependency? It's really robbing both individual's identities. It can create a tangled web of sorrow, confusion and fear, which is certainly not God's plans for either person's life.

Proverbs 19:19 *A man of great wrath shall suffer punishment: for if thou deliver him, yet thou must do it again.*

If we are always rescuing people from their situation because we don't want them to suffer discomfort, Proverbs says that you will have to do it again, and again, and again. How many times did you pay that overextended credit card bill, or bail someone out of jail, or keep paying for rehab or even something simple like picking up someone's dirty laundry, only to find yourself doing it over and over? Meanwhile, the other person is getting the "Out of Jail Free" card and you find yourself angrier and angrier.

My husband Rick, says something very powerful to meditate on, and that is: "We train people how to treat us." It is only when that person has to begin to take full

Keep Walking...

responsibility for their behavior that they learn about the consequences. It is then up to them to decide if they want to change or keep receiving the ramifications of their actions. We must allow it if we want them to change!! When we continue to bail them out, it harms the relationship in the end and everyone gets changed for the worse.

Ecclesiastes 8:11 *Because sentence against an evil work is not executed speedily, therefore the heart of the sons of men is fully set in them to do evil.*

Only if the judicial system would get this scripture, I think there would be far less crime. Other countries (probably not even Christian) do this much better than the United States. We keep letting people get around their punishment, whatever it is, because they have the best lawyers or the most money or a friend in the system, etc., releasing them back into society to possibly do much greater destruction.

I encourage you that sympathy is a great thing and coming alongside others can bring great relief and comfort. However, it is not intended for long-term use. Check your own fears if you find yourself in these situations. We need to let people go through the fire but continue to represent the Living God to them, and continue in prayer for them so that the hurt, destruction and anger will have a much shorter course.

My new favorite saying about fire is that it destroys the destructible and purifies the indestructible—those things in us of God. Don't be afraid of the fire!!

Keep burning...

Good Cheer

It seems as though many of God's most precious people are walking through difficult times. First of all we need to know that tribulations are a part of this life, but praise God, He has given us the power to live through it all, with good cheer.

John 16:33 *These things I have spoken unto you, that in me ye might have peace. In the world ye shall have tribulation: but be of good cheer; I have overcome the world.*

Jesus very words were that, "in me," there is good cheer and peace during the tribulations of the world.

The best part of that verse is the word "have overcome" which is past tense. We can be at peace and have joy because we are operating from a position of completed victory. Rick said something profound on the call the other day that is worth mentioning. He stated that we are always trying to get to a place of victory, when in reality we should be standing and starting and moving forward from a position of victory. I think the verse in John 16 verifies that. In Mary Pat language, if everything you need has already been provided for, peace and cheer should be a normal part of living in the trials. Again, a position of victory. Starting out in victory should make the battle much easier to handle.

Wrap your head around that and it will change your life. I can then ask the question, "Why do we have to go through tribulations?" Many love the blessed, prosperity, grace message much better! It's all about becoming blessed, healed prosperous, great family unity, and all things well, when in reality God says something very different.

Keep Walking...

2 Corinthians 1:4 *Who comforteth us in all our tribulation, that we may be able to comfort them which are in any trouble, by the comfort wherewith we ourselves are comforted of God.*

Our tribulations are about God showing us His great comfort (if we will let Him) so that we can comfort others who are going through a similar trial. In other words, our tribulations produce fruit, and fruit is not just for us, but for others to feed upon and grow.

So often we pray and pray about God using us to serve Him, but we prefer it in a grandiose and mighty way with no sweat. God's cycle seems to be: trials and tribulations, pressing into Him, Him purifying us to look more like Him, gratitude and praise for bringing us through and then sharing with others. Only to start the process again.

Maybe our prayers should be "Lord - I trust that you are in this fire. You are destroying the destructible and purifying the indestructible. If I can believe that, I will emerge without the smell of smoke or singed hair, and be used by you as a pure vessel of honor for others."

The devil would just as soon have us come out with burnt hair, smelling like destruction and defeat and a countenance to match. Uh, not sure where God would get the glory He deserves, when the world sees a beat up ragamuffin. The best form of evangelism is going through tough times with the comfort and grace of God, having peace and cheer that the world totally can't understand. When they ask what drugs I am taking, I have one answer - the Gos-pill. A seed just got planted in that person's life of the mighty God that we serve.

Has overcome...

Family Time

As I pondered on this message, I decided to focus on the many people who will be spending time with family members during the holidays. The enemy sure seems to be able to get things stirred up at this time of year. With that in mind, I thought I would focus on Romans chapter 14. In fact, that is your assignment, to read the whole thing before the front door opens and all the different family members come together. It might just save you (and others) a boat load of frustration and agitation, not to mention indigestion. Here are a few worthy excerpts taken from either the KJV or the Amplified Bible.

Opening Scene - Thanksgiving or any other "family" day.

Romans 14:1 (AMP) *As for the man who is a weak believer, welcome him (into your fellowship), but not to criticize his opinions or pass judgment on his scruples or perplex him with discussions.*

Scene 2 -Dinner time

Romans 14:2-3 *For one believeth that he may eat all things: another, who is weak, eateth herbs. Let not him that eateth despise him that eateth not; and let not him which eateth not judge him that eateth: for God hath received him.*

Scene 3 -Dinner conversation

Romans 14:10 (AMP) *Why do you criticize and pass judgment on your brother? Or you, why do you look down upon or despise your brother? For we shall all stand before the judgment seat of God.*

Romans 14:13 (AMP) *Then let us no more criticize and blame and pass judgment on one another, but rather de-*

Keep Walking...

cide and endeavor never to put a stumbling block or an obstacle or a hindrance in the way of a brother.

<u>Scene 4 - God's plan</u> (enters in front, back and side doors)

Romans 14:19 (AMP) *So let us then definitely aim for and eagerly pursue what makes for harmony and for mutual upbuilding (edification and development) of one another.*

<u>Closing scene</u> - All holidays (and any other day for that matter)

Romans 14:17-18 *For the kingdom of God is not meat and drink; but righteousness, and peace, and joy in the Holy Ghost. For he that in these things serveth Christ is acceptable to God, and approved of men.*

Again, I ask you to read the whole chapter of Romans 14. Many of our family members are barely saved and verse 10 explains that Christian are not to judge each other with reference to the practice of morally neutral issues (which is a holiday conversation). We are each responsible to God and the right of judgment belongs to HIM! Weak and strong Christians shall all stand, not at each other's judgment , but before the judgment seat of Christ. Playing God has long hours, no benefits and a lot of tough work.

This holiday season, leave the judging of others to Christ. You will be amazed at the peace that comes when we let Him do His job and we sit back and enjoy His peace while obeying His word!

No judging...

WHAT A DEAL

Hope you are having an "Oh, Happy Day"—if not—why not? Happy days are all by faith and sometimes that means we can't see it yet. But if we are walking in faith, we just believe that "this is the day the Lord hath made and I will rejoice in it"

Many of us have loved the scripture from Zephaniah whereby we hear the good news that God is singing songs and rejoicing over us. I want to look at another part of this scripture and how it screams (in a nice way!!) of how much God loves us and accepts us just like we are.

Zephaniah 3:17 *The LORD thy God in the midst of thee is mighty; he will save, he will rejoice over thee with joy; he will rest in his love, he will joy over thee with singing.*

The part where it says that "he will rest in his love" is worth a good look. One of the definitions of this word "rest" in the Hebrew language means "to be silent, to let alone; hence (by implication) to be deaf—leave off speaking, hold his peace."

Here's how the Amplified states this verse:

Zephaniah 3:17 *The Lord your God is in the mist of you, a Mighty One, a Savior (Who saves)! He will rejoice over you with joy; He will rest (in silent satisfaction) and in His love He will be silent and make no mention (of past sins, or even recall them); He will exult over you with singing.*

This verse could perhaps be one of the most powerful verses that introduce us to the New Testament... The Good News! Let's do a quick Hebrew language summary (Mary Pat style) of verse 17.

The Lord your God is in the midst of you and is mighty. The "midst" means the closest part of you and "mighty"

239   *Keep Walking...*

is a powerful, warrior, champion. So everything you need to be an overcomer, to win the race, to be victorious, is at the closest part of you!

Next, If we would totally open ourselves wide to Him, we can have the gift of salvation and freedom... period.

When we do just that, He then rejoices over us with joy. God will be "bright and cheerful" over us.

He then reminds us that if we will receive Him, He will be silent and not make any mention of our sins. Now that is an extremely decent and generous offer and promise!! A "chance of a lifetime" offer. Now we know where TV gets its marketing material!!

Finally, He will "spin around" with shouts of joy over us. God sings all the time and it is over us. Not only does He sing joy over us, He sings songs of deliverance (Hebrew - escape) over us.

Psalm 32:7 *Thou art my hiding place; thou shalt preserve me from trouble; thou shalt compass me about with songs of deliverance. Selah.*

This is a deal of a lifetime. I only hope that we focus on this one, believe in it, receive it and pass it on.

Tune into His songs...

NOT MY BATTLE

I was reading Psalms 18 this morning and noticed how many times David was very aware that it was God who had done everything he needed during this battle for his life. The scene is David speaking to the Lord who had delivered him from the hand of all his enemies and from the hand of Saul.

Read Psalms 18 and count how many times David says "He" (God) or "Thou" (God) did stuff. I am not guaranteeing that I counted correctly, but in 50 verses, I counted David acknowledging God doing all the work in keeping David from harm and delivering him 31 times. What if we could come to the conclusion that it is not what we do, but what He is doing all the time for us? One scripture comes to mind to summarize that thought:

2 Chronicles 20:15 *And he said, Hearken ye, all Judah, and ye inhabitants of Jerusalem, and thou king Jehoshaphat, Thus saith the LORD unto you, Be not afraid nor dismayed by reason of this great multitude; for the battle is not yours, but God's.*

When we praise and acknowledge God we are throwing the spotlight on Him. The more we put the spotlight on Him, the more He causes us to shine. Modern medicine attests to the value of bringing a depressed person into a brightly lit room, and how it helps heal depression. How much more will praise and focus for all that He does for us bring forth the light and power of God into our lives? The following are a few of my favorite verses from Psalm 18 that bring home this point:

Psalm 18:19 *He brought me forth also into a large place; he delivered me, because he delighted in me.*

Keep Walking...

Psalm 18:28 *For thou wilt light my candle: the LORD my God will enlighten my darkness.*

Psalm 18:32 *It is God that girdeth me with strength, and maketh my way perfect.*

I don't think I need to do the "Hebrew" word thing. Simply meditate on all that God does for us by reading all of Psalms 18 and underlining all the "He and Thou" words. Go on vacation from trying to fight all your battles. God is up for it all the time!!

Let God light your candle...

My Growing Family

I just celebrated my birthday and even though my day started out way out of kilter, followed by the dreaded thought of going to work and doing inventory in a zero degree freezer, I was able to make a comment on Facebook that I want to share:

"I am overwhelmed by all the birthday wishes. When I lost my kids, my mom, and my sister, my family felt like it was getting frightfully small. As Beth Moore said, "When you are a believer, your family never shrinks, but only grows." I so see that now and am forever grateful!! Just glad I don't have to cook for them all!!

That comment by Beth Moore ministered to me more than you can imagine. So much loss was almost suffocating. It was like everything became "minimal." Holidays would have "minimal" family members around the table, family phone calls would be "minimal," happy family pictures would be "minimal" and on and on.

However, Beth Moore was really right on with her comment, especially when I found scriptures that supported it:

Ephesians 3:14 *For this cause I bow my knees unto the Father of our Lord Jesus Christ.*

Ephesians 3:15 *Of whom the whole family in heaven and earth is named.*

I must say I feel like there is more of my family in heaven than on earth at this point. So you see, if you feel like you are the only one left, that is simply a lie if you are a believer. I have "adopted" kids, and more and more people who love me like family than I ever had with my "genetic" family!!

Keep Walking...

If you are a born again child of God, then you have the blood of Jesus running through your veins and we are all related as one big, interesting family!!

Oh, by the way, my birthday day did get turned around. Who would have thought that God would bring back my peace and joy in a freezer full of beef. Only God!!

Later family...

Jonah Knows Best....Not!

I am always grateful for the opportunity to share the Living Power of God in my life. It's called a testimony. It's really all we have to truly share with others, so "don't despise the small beginnings," AKA, the really crazy, wild stuff that you may have done. God uses all of it and doesn't waste anything we've been through either by circumstances or our own choices. Embrace the life that you have lived, bundle it up and lay it at the feet of the Cross. God can do great things with our mess if we allow Him.

Job 8:7 *Though thy beginning was small, yet thy latter end should greatly increase.*

I recently started studying the book of Jonah. The book was penned to emphasize that God loves all people and desires to show them mercy based upon repentance. Jonah was having issues with God, when called to go preach to the Assyrians, who were dreaded and hated because of their persecution of Israel. He was to preach repentance and a promise of God's mercy if they responded to the sent Word; otherwise God would bring on them great judgment.

Jonah's issues stemmed from his religious pride of wondering why God would have mercy on people who had abused Israel. He was forgetting all along that Israel had been charged with revealing the message of forgiveness and mercy. God had declared that all nations of the Earth would be blessed through the Abrahamic covenant.

Genesis 12:2-3 *And I will make of thee a great nation, and I will bless thee, and make thy name great; and thou shalt be a blessing: And I will bless them that bless thee, and curse him that curseth thee: and in thee shall all families of the earth be blessed.*

Keep Walking...

Jonah knew that if the Assyrians of Ninevah repented, and God spared them, that they would be free to plunder and pillage Israel again. This nationalistic patriotism and his disdain that mercy would be offered to non-covenant people, prompted Jonah to try to get away from the Spirit of Prophecy that was on him. He thought that if he ran away, the presence of the Lord would not follow him. Oh, Jonah—don't ya know?

To speed up this story, God hurled out a great wind and storm that caused circumstances to bring Jonah face-to-face with his missionary call. God then prepared a giant fish to swallow Jonah and live for three days amidst giant-fish, gastric juices, seaweed, and lots of other little critters that whales swallow. Finally, Jonah, after surviving whale, projectile vomiting onto land, went and shared the message, to which the Assyrians responded positively. This really bummed him out and he decided to believe that perhaps their repentance wasn't genuine or that God would choose another strategy. He thus decided to camp out and wait for the appointed day of judgment.

God used this waiting time to teach Jonah a valuable lesson. God prepared a giant plant to grow overnight and provide shade. Jonah rejoiced in his good fortune. Then God prepared a worm to chew up the plant and cause it to wither. God then sent a dry, hot wind to intensify the heat that Jonah was experiencing. Jonah lamented and expressed his displeasure to God. God responded by showing the inconsistency of being concerned for a gourd, but being totally unconcerned about the fate of the inhabitants of Nineveh whom God loved.

God was doing a deep and profound work in Jonah's life as well as showing His great glory to a whole nation. He orchestrated events to make it happen. When unfortunate events happen in our lives we often begin rebuking the devil thinking that it is he that is causing all these issues, when it might not be him after all, but a Living God accomplishing His work through us. God's ways are higher than ours and often that includes necessary, albeit uncomfortable situations.

Don't worry so much about what is going on in your life, always trying to figure out whether it is Satan, God or our own weird choices. In all three circumstances, the best thing we can do is draw ever closer to God. In thinking that Satan is involved in all tough times, we may just be rebuking the best thing God is trying to do in us, in others, and even nations. Allow God to catapult you out of your comfort zone and into His greatest glory!

Catapulting can be great.

NO STUFF

If I had to pick a favorite holiday for its meaning, it would be Thanksgiving. Mostly because it covers all the other days—a grateful heart for God and His love through Jesus, who came to show me that I could walk for the glory of God on earth, if I would know Him.

I never really know what I am going to put in a message, but through reading and praying, I ask God to give me something that will minister to at least one person. Today it was the first thing I read in the book of Micah.

Micah 6:7-8 *⁷Will the LORD be pleased with thousands of rams, or with ten thousands of rivers of oil? shall I give my firstborn for my transgression, the fruit of my body for the sin of my soul? ⁸He hath shewed thee, O man, what is good; and what doth the LORD require of thee, but to do justly, and to love mercy, and to walk humbly with thy God?*

Here we have the 613 laws condensed into three. In this chapter, God is pressing charges in a lawsuit against His people. If we look at verse 7, we see them trying to buy Him off with extravagant offerings and impressive gifts. In verse 8, in a sense, God is saying that He is not interested in their stuff. It's so plain and simple. He is telling them that there can be no substitute for love and loyalty and fair dealing; that nothing is acceptable unless one is in a proper relationship with God and his neighbor (sounds like the new covenant!!).

Remain honest in all you do, cherish compassionate faithfulness, and commit yourself to live in submission to God, is what He is saying to His people. I do not see one requirement for religious activity, but only a belief in Jesus Christ. We keep trusting spiritual gymnastics rather than His life in us.

Keep Walking..

John 15:5 *I am the vine, ye are the branches: He that abideth in me, and I in him, the same bringeth forth much fruit: for without me ye can do nothing.*

It is in Him and through Him that we can "walk humbly with God." Here we are "walking" again. So simple, so profound, so full, but yet so hard. We will do every other thing we can think of, except simply walk with God. God isn't requiring anything else. If we are walking with Him, we are going in a perfect direction.

Psalm 37:23 *The steps of a good man are ordered by the LORD: and he delighteth in his way.*

Psalm 37:31 *The law of his God is in his heart; none of his steps shall slide.*

Keep walking (imagine that!)

BE BLESSED

September and October could be a very depressing time for me. These were the months of the loss of my two children, mom and sister. It doesn't, however, change the fact that I am blessed. I often sign emails, etc., as "Be blessed" and then in parenthesis I put "Cause you are anyway."

If you are a believer you are blessed and I am going to prove it to you. Even though you may not feel like it, I assure you, you are. You might as well receive it, walk in it, and let it manifest in your life.

Psalm 109:17 *As he loved cursing, so let it come unto him: as he delighted not in blessing, so let it be far from him.*

In reading this verse this morning, I was moved about how important it is for me to "delight" in God's blessings for me, lest they be far from manifesting in my life. This prompted me to study about being blessed. First, let me share the Hebrew and Greek definitions of the word blessed, so you can really see the true meaning.

In the Hebrew it means "happiness" but comes from a root word meaning "to be straight, lead, to go forward, to be prospered and relieved."

In the Greek it means "supremely blessed, fortunate, well thought of, and happy."

The word "blessed" is the object of God's favor and reasons for this are as follows:

1. <u>We are chosen:</u>
   Ephesians 1:3 *Blessed be the God and Father of our Lord Jesus Christ, who hath blessed us with all spiritual blessings in heavenly places in Christ:*

Keep Walking..

2. We believe:
   Galatians 3:9 *So then they which be of faith are blessed with faithful Abraham.*

3. We are forgiven:
   Psalm 32:1-2 *Blessed is he whose transgression is forgiven, whose sin is covered. Blessed is the man unto whom the LORD imputeth not iniquity, and in whose spirit there is no guile.*

4. We are justified (just like it didn't happen!):
   Romans 4:6 *Even as David also describeth the blessedness of the man, unto whom God imputeth righteousness without works,* **Romans 4:7** *Saying, Blessed are they whose iniquities are forgiven, and whose sins are covered.*

5. We are chastened:
   Psalm 94:12 *Blessed is the man whom thou chastenest, O LORD, and teachest him out of thy law;*

6. We keep God's Word:
   Revelation 1:3 *Blessed is he that readeth, and they that hear the words of this prophecy, and keep those things which are written therein: for the time is at hand.*

With this in mind, I think I would like to try and summarize this by praying:

"Heavenly Father, first of all forgive me for thinking that I am blessed because I have worked at being good and that I am the cause of my blessings. Let me realize that I am being led and prospering as the object of Your favor because You chose me from the foundation of the world and I said yes. Lord I trust in You and Your promises by faith, even when I can't see a physical manifestation and because of that, You tell me I am blessed.

Keep Walking...

Father, I am blessed because I am forgiven, just like I never sinned (justified); you chasten and teach me instead of dreading it. I can now see that it is a part of the blessing. Lord, help me to be hungry for your word knowing that nothing else will satisfy me until I do. I thank You that blessings are not about me, but about You. If I am born again, I am blessed. Let me act like it, so I can reflect more of You. In Jesus name. Amen."

Be blessed (because you are anyway!).

SHEPHERDS AND SHEEP

Greetings to all. I often say that in life, we are all shepherds and sheep. We might only be a shepherd over our small dog, or maybe our families, or at work, or even a whole country. However no matter how "big" of a shepherd we may be, we are also all sheep. We are all "under" someone. I might run a big company, but I am still under the watchful eye of the Board of Directors. I might be a sheep as a small child, under the care of a parent, but still a shepherd over a fish in a fish bowl. And of course we are all sheep under the watchful eye of Jehovah Roti (Psalm 23:1).

The point is we all need to be examples of Christ, The Great Shepherd, being good leaders of whatever we might be over. We see washing the feet of His disciples in these passages:

John 13:14-15 *If I then, your Lord and Master, have washed your feet; ye also ought to wash one another's feet. For I have given you an example, that ye should do as I have done to you.*

John 13:17 *If ye know these things, happy are ye if ye do them.*

If we will serve one another in whatever leadership position we find ourselves, then we will be supremely blessed (Greek =happy) according to John 13:17. Jesus' lifestyle and teachings establish the mode of a servant leader. A servant leader leads from a position of personal security, knowing who God has made him or her to be, and resting in the peaceful awareness and confidence that God's hand is ordering their personal destiny. That person knows his identity in Christ and starts from a place of victory rather than trying to get to a place of victory.

Keep Walking...

The godly, servant leader is one who stoops to help another, who counts others better than himself (Phil 2:3-4), who lays down his life for others (John 10:11), and who seeks to serve rather than be served (Luke 22:27). Until a person is ready to wash dirty feet, he is not qualified to be a kingdom leader.

Now we can all certainly muster up a good show and wash someone's feet, but it really will not produce any fruit. Serving is a heart thing, not a doing thing. We can only serve at this level when we allow our identity in Christ to be received and then given away. There is a tremendous humility that manifests in our ability to lead as Jesus did. Trust me, the whole world will notice.

I pray for our leaders/shepherds in our country. Oh, what a difference it would make, if they would become servant leaders, serving the people of this country. In the meantime, I will keep my eye on this Jesus. He was the greatest Shepherd of all times by simply caring for and being willing to "pick out" all our imperfections/sins, and clean us up with His grace and mercy. It only requires a "yes" from us. With that, God can mold us all into becoming great servant leaders or simply awesome shepherds, no matter the size of the "flock."

From a tiny fish to a whole country, God is calling for greatness. Let it begin with you in your arena of leadership.

Keep serving...

Breaking Co-Dependency

I want to talk about the term co-dependency from a biblical standpoint (like there should be any other??) Maybe your marriage is falling apart, or your children, or neighbors are really taking advantage of you, but you convince yourself that it really is normal and nothing is wrong. Well, Jesus had the same problem.

If you read all of Luke 24, you find that Jesus has died, and the disciples on the road to Emmaus are disappointed and sad that this "Jesus" didn't end up being there to make their life easier—or so it seemed. I remember when I was studying about grief and sadness that the scripture Luke 24:17 found Jesus (unbeknownst to the disciples) asking them "why were they so sad?" It was simply because they had "heard" only what they wanted to hear and missed the deepest, most profound message, that had ever been taught. They heard about the Savior/King part but somehow missed the suffering chapter. Isn't that what we always do? We often pretend things are getting better only to miss the suffering part that we or others must go through to get God's best. Let me (or rather the Word) explain:

Luke 24:25-26 *Then he said unto them, O fools, and slow of heart to believe all that the prophets have spoken: Ought not Christ to have suffered these things, and to enter into his glory?*

Jesus had told his disciples over and over that He would suffer and die, but they didn't "hear" that part. On the road to Emmaus, He is chastising them. Their spiritual dullness had come from a failure to recognize that the scriptures had foretold the necessity of the Messiah's suffering. He had to suffer before entering into His glory. We, or others, may have to suffer to enter the full manifestation of God in our lives as well. It's kinda part of the deal as disciples.

Keep Walking...

Perhaps we are disappointed in the outcome of our prayers for situations because we don't want ourselves, or others, to suffer in any way, shape or form. We don't follow the prompting of the Holy Spirit to not bail that son out of jail, or not allow that alcoholic to use you to cover up for them, or quit doing for someone what they are well capable of doing themselves. We don't want them to suffer, so we prevent it. But the suffering might be the very thing that catapults them into a deep and vibrant relationship with Christ and "forces" them to finally grow up and be who God has called them to be.

When I was going through what seemed a never-ending pit of suffering, I grabbed hold of the message of Christ. Not just the good, sugar-coated part, but the discipleship part as well. Disciples follow their Master. That might mean a few miles through some rough times. Don't despise the difficulties, just follow the King, and guaranteed, He will bring you out on the other side.

If I had to sum up the life of Christ in a few words, it would be that He woke up every morning knowing He was facing the most horrific death. Regardless, He prayed, and taught, and ate fish and figs. The greatest news is that He walked towards death and came out on the other side. He showed us it can be done and how to do it. Simply follow Him.

Keep following...

CATAPULTING OUT OF YOUR COMFORT ZONE

What exactly is "living for the glory of God?" We often say many things like, "Glory to God; I'm living for the glory of God; God be the glory." We hear it on Christian TV, out of our own mouths and certainly at church, but do we really understand what we are saying? God is ultimate and everything else is not. Until we get that order straight, everything else will be a rival for God's glory. Giving God glory is much about us! The glory of God is the manifestation of His Truth, His worth, His beauty and His greatness through us.

Remember the song "Cover the Earth with His Glory?" It sounds great, right? But God does not have a big pitcher of glory that He is going to pour out on us so that we can take a big glory bath and have a wonderful spiritual spa moment. His glory is poured out through us representing Him. The sound of heaven should be coming through our mouths and our actions to represent Him.

We are all conduits of God's glory if we allow it. God's glory is huge and it is going to take all of us to manifest our part on the earth. We are like telescopes taking something unbelievably big and trying to bring it into focus so others can begin to see Him. Will you be the lens that God can use to bring His greatness into a place that people can taste and begin to digest His majesty?

Psalm 34:8 *O taste and see that the LORD is good: blessed is the man that trusteth in him.*

Be a spoonful of glory and soon the whole world may see the greatness of God through His trusted servants.

Choose the largest spoon.

(Song - "Cover the Earth," by Israel Houghton)

Keep Walking...

Brain Power

I tried to make a gratitude list in my head, but it never seems to articulate what I want to say. Somehow words aren't enough or seem too trite. I end up say things like "I am thankful for my husband, or my beautiful property, or my health," and on and on, but the words just never seem deep enough or wide enough to capture how I feel about it all.

I was pondering on that again today, and it really reminded me of my thoughts about God. They simply aren't big enough!! I can't seem to wrap my head around Him—He is awe and a wonder. They say we only use about 10% of our brains here on earth. I wonder if God is saving the other 90% so when we get to heaven we can really "take" Him all in. I know I will need all the brain space I can get to take in His significance.

As I often do, I also am taking in what Oswald Chambers (devotional book) has been talking about. Allow me to share some of his excerpts:

- "It is shallow nonsense to say that God forgives us because He is love... The love of God means Calvary - nothing less... The only basis for which God can forgive me is the Cross of Christ."

- "Beware of the pleasant view of the fatherhood of God: God is so kind and loving that of course He will forgive us. That thought, based solely on emotion, cannot be found anywhere in the New Testament. The only basis on which God can forgive us is the tremendous tragedy of the Cross of Christ."

- Never build your case for forgiveness on the idea that God is our Father and He will forgive us because He loves us... It makes the Cross unnecessary and the redemption "much ado about nothing."

Keep Walking..

- "God forgives sin only because of the death of Christ...The greatest note of triumph ever sounded in the ears of a startled universe was that sounded on the Cross of Christ - "It is finished!"

I can wrap my head around the emotional things like, "He forgives me of my sin because He loves me," but to associate death with love, again, is more than my humanness can sometimes handle.

It is with that, that I am simply and profoundly grateful. There are no words to really grasp this, only a heart of faith and belief in The One that made it all possible to walk on this earth without condemnation, guilt, sickness, sorrow, pain, loss, brokenness and on, and on. You may say that you have many of these things, but I promise when Jesus took His last breath and said it was finished, He was 100% correct. It is finished, and if you believe in Him, then at this very moment, there is healing and hope.

Keep appropriating what He accomplished for you and me. Look for it, breath it, speak it, and never, ever give up. God is doing a mighty work in every situation -- if we can only believe!!

Psalm 84:5-7 *Blessed is the man whose strength is in You, Whose heart is set on pilgrimage. As they pass through the Valley of Baca (weeping). They make it a spring; The rain also covers it with pools (blessings). They go from strength to strength; each one appears before God in Zion. (NKJV)*

The first usage of the word "strength" means praise, boldness, loud. The second and third times it means army, virtue, valor.

May I be so bold to translate this in "Mary Pat" language? "Blessed and extremely joyful is the person who praises you boldly and loudly. As we walk through

Keep Walking...

tough times "praising the Power down," dry places begin to provide living water, and new seeds sprout.

The army of God carries us through and before we know it, we are before the Living God. Hallelujah!!!"

Okay pilgrims - keep walking!!

YOUR TASTE

Let's face it, we all have had plans for how our lives should be. When some trauma, big decision or a huge change in our life occurs, our well thought-out plans can go down the drain and suck us down with them if we allow it. There are forks in the road that everyone faces throughout their lives. We can choose the direction that causes us to persevere, accept the situation for what it is, keep walking through it (think Psalm 23:4) and come out on the other side. Or we can choose the direction that has us setting up camp in our "unplanned plans," denying that things are changed and therefore becoming depressed, conflicted and hopeless.

We can doubt that God even exists or we can choose unquestionable faith and ask God to help our unbelief (Mark 9:24). We can also choose to be "exceedingly joyful in our tribulations" as Paul did (2 Corinthians 7:4). (Answer = best choice, need God's help!)

2 Corinthians 7:4 *Great is my boldness of speech toward you, great is my glorying of you: I am filled with comfort, I am exceeding joyful in all our tribulation.*

Another slippery-slope option when your world falls apart, is self-pity, which masquerades as compassion for one's self and can quickly become addictive. In traumas and losses, the world would say you were entitled to poor, sad, long days, too much to drink or other ungodly things. But as believers we must be able to discern between taking good, kind, loving care of ourselves and self-indulgence.

When you retreat into self-pity, you park, or worse, you go downhill. Jesus always looked outward and not at His own circumstances.

Keep Walking...

He is our guide on how to handle life. As far as death, we know that if we stick with God, it isn't even an option!

John 8:52 *If a man keep my saying, he shall never taste of death.*

Choose your "taste" wisely.

How do you Labor?

As we prepare to celebrate Labor Day, I thought it might be wise to see how the Bible defines labor. The Greek language is so rich. The English language is limited and we can get fooled when we apply the English definition to words.

Hebrews 6:10 *For God is not unrighteous to forget your work and labour of love, which ye have shewed toward his name, in that ye have ministered to the saints, and do minister.*

Hebrews 4:11 *Let us labour therefore to enter into that rest, lest any man fall after the same example of unbelief.*

Here we have the word labor in two different scriptures. The first one, in Hebrews 6:10, means to work hard and become fatigued. I think most of us have that one down pretty good, especially when you are trying to love people. It is hard work because the word "labour" in this passage really comes from doing it in our own strength.

In Hebrews 4:11, the word "labour" means something totally different. It is a spiritual word if you will. It means to use speed, to make an earnest effort, to be diligent, to study. I always thought it was an interesting concept to "labor to rest;" it seems like such an oxymoron. I do get it however, because for me it is hard work to rest. But here we have God encouraging us to press in to all the work that He accomplished on the Cross, instead of us trying to do it in our own strength.

The Cross accomplished everything. Jesus is righteousness, provision, healing, peace, victory and deliverance for every situation. Our problem is we look at everything through natural eyes instead of spiritual eyes. That is the main reason we don't understand God.

Keep Walking...

God says we are healed and our physical bodies say otherwise. We thus get confused, doubt God and move on, trying to find something else that will work. We move away from God, instead of pressing into Him in belief that healing is coming our way.

What if we made an "earnest effort, studied and were diligent" to enter into that rest of the finished work of Christ, instead of trying to figure how to hurry up and get ourselves healed. I think it is worth a try. After all, that is really what being a Christian is—trusting and believing in the death, burial and resurrection of Jesus Christ. This death, burial and resurrection is exactly what we need for every situation and circumstance in our lives. Plant that deadly thing in your life and labor to rest in Jesus. You might just find that resurrection and new life will occur!

Labor to rest...

Choices

I feel a deep and gnawing concern for where we are in this period of time. We should give our full focus to the Word of God.

Jeremiah 7:8 *Behold, ye trust in lying words, that cannot profit.*

Jeremiah 7:23-24 *But this thing commanded I them, saying, Obey my voice, and I will be your God, and ye shall be my people: and walk ye in all the ways that I have commanded you, that it may be well unto you. (24) But they hearkened not, nor inclined their ear, but walked in the counsels and in the imagination of their evil heart, and went backward, and not forward.*

Here we have God telling Jeremiah to tell the Israelites that they preferred listening to lying prophets and worshiping idols versus strengthening their relationship with, and "hearkening" to, Him. He is a jealous God and is going to have none of that. There is a price for this disobedience. These Israelites are no different than we are today. We want to listen to what we want to hear, what feels the best to our senses, and fits into our own self-devised plans.

God was speaking through Jeremiah that he was not be a "part of the crowd," but instead a voice used by God of judgment against sin, namely idolatry and false prophets. Jeremiah continued to encourage them to obey and turn back to Him, but they refused. I lost count of how many times God told Jeremiah NOT to pray for these chosen people, but here is one verse:

Jeremiah 7:16 *Therefore pray not thou for this people, neither lift up cry nor prayer for them, neither make intercession to me: for I will not hear thee.*

Keep Walking...

Let me summarize the two main things that are on my heart from these scriptures:

First, lies never profit and truth always profits. Apply that to what is going on all around you in this country and pray for discernment. Don't get tempted to join in the lie, willingly or unwillingly, so that your life will be more comfortable. Take a stand, be as bold as the disciples were in Acts 4.

Acts 4:29-31 *And now, Lord, behold their threatenings: and grant unto thy servants, that with all boldness they may speak thy word, By stretching forth thine hand to heal; and that signs and wonders may be done by the name of thy holy child Jesus. And when they had prayed, the place was shaken where they were assembled together; and they were all filled with the Holy Ghost, and they spake the word of God with boldness.*

Secondly, if we do not pay attention to what the Word of God says, and prefer the easier more comfortable way, then we will walk backward, not forward (vs. 24 above).

I love (well.. sometimes) that God lets us choose. He is very gracious to lay the options before us, nothing hidden, all out in the open. Don't be a fool and pick what you consider to be the easier way. If you are going backward, then you are probably following your own way. If you are prospering in your faith and spiritual life, then you are trusting in Truth.

Choose Him every time...

BIRTHING ISHMAELS?

When Christ is in you, you should be good, because He is good!

I have finished rereading a book by John Bevere called "Thus Saith the Lord." It is a book on how to discern between true prophecy from God or from a man tickling your ears. I highly recommend reading this book during this time of deception. Remember, the Word says that if possible, even the elect will be deceived. It is up to us to keep our minds and heart in the Word so we know if what we hear is truly from the heart of God. All good and uplifting words are not from Him.

Matthew 24:24 *For there shall arise false Christs, and false prophets, and shall shew great signs and wonders; insomuch that, if it were possible, they shall deceive the very elect.*

With that said, I want to share a quote from the last page of "Thus Saith the Lord."

"Our culture is not trained to wait and let God work. We are inbred with, "If we don't have it, find a way to get it." So if we don't have the money to buy it, charge it. If sickness strikes, why pray? We call the doctor- we have insurance. If we have been give a promise from God, go for it. Tell everyone. Proclaim it, and through a little manipulation and/or control we can get it. (of course we don't say the last part.) Then we proclaim God fulfilled His promise to us. But in reality we have just birthed another Ishmael."

The last half of this quote really woke me up. How often do we hear someone say, "I prayed for a car as I needed to get to work," and everywhere they went for the next few days, church, work, Facebook, etc., they shared they needed a car. And lo and behold, they get

Keep Walking...

a car. Praise God that my prayer has been answered. God is so good." I hear it all the time, "I prayed for what I wanted and got it." Did they pray and then help God with the answer? Abraham certainly did when he helped God fulfill God's promise to him by sleeping with Hagar and having Ishmael.

"But in reality we have just birthed another Ishmael."

I am going to end this newsletter and let the Holy Spirit show us where we think God has answered our prayers but in reality, we made it happen ourselves. And with that, we know there will be problems to come.

John 15:5 *I am the vine, ye are the branches: He that abideth in me, and I in him, the same bringeth forth much fruit: for without me ye can do nothing.*

Lord, please help me realize when I seek you, but then add my own efforts, manipulation, and control that it was not your work, but mine. You get no glory from that and I perhaps have limited your best. I want only you and your timing for everything in my life. For without you, I can do nothing!

Less of me...

WHO IS HELPING YOU?

Spring is around the corner and that means lots of work outside. March is my favorite time of the year. Everything gets planted and then God does what only He can do, and that is to make things grow providing us with food and flowers and bright things!

I thought today would be a good time to share some things to reaffirm our need to fully submit to God. Remember, whatever or whoever we submit to, or serve, has to take care of us.

Deuteronomy 32:37-38 *And he shall say, Where are their gods, their rock in whom they trusted, Which did eat the fat of their sacrifices, and drank the wine of their drink offerings? Let them rise up and help you, and be your protection.*

Satan doesn't get us to follow him by coming in with his sprouted horns, wearing a weird, red outfit and carrying a pitchfork. We are smarter than that. The Bible says he is a wolf in sheep's clothing. In other words, he doesn't dress for us to recognize him, thus we are easily deceived. He is a master at fanning our pride and getting us involved in handling life our own way. We then resist God, and by default draw near to Satan.

Here is how Beth Moore succinctly puts it:

"Satan doesn't have to convince you and me to do his will for our life. He only has to tempt us to demand our own way. God has something bigger for each of us that our human minds can hug. Something eternal. Something that will still matter when our bones have turned to heaps of dust. God knows everything about you and every matter concerning you. Nothing is hidden from His sight. So submit to God. He is always looking for our ultimate good and takes your hurts personally. So

Keep Walking...

submit to God. He is holy and incapable of abusing His divine authority over you. So submit to God. He knows when your motive was right but your mouth messed up. So submit to God. He knows exactly how to work terrible into good. So submit to God. He loves you completely and unconditionally and will never let you go. So submit to God. He knows the well-deliberated plan for your lives and how all things must fall into place for you to fulfill your destiny. So submit to God, He will never put to shame those who trust in Him. So submit to God. The devil is trying to steal from you, and destroy you, and make it look like it was all your idea."

I don't know about you, but I have handed over enough of my life to that punk. It is up to me to humbly submit to God and know that He has my back in every situation. We know pride brings destruction; my own way brings destruction. Today I pray for humility and once again—His way!

No deception...

Love the One You're With

It seems as if I am on a roll with songs and music lately. Rick and I listened to old tunes when driving back from Florida and one keeps rolling around in my mind as a "significant nugget" of God's truth. I guess the real message in the song is contentment. So often I wish I were with someone else, or would rather be doing anything with anyone other than the one I happen to be with at the time. If we did take the old "rock and roll" message of, "If you can't be with the one you love, love the one your with," doo, doo, doo, doo! (That was part of the song haha!), it can also enter into the grief and loss process for me. If I can't be with Forrest, Dustin, Mom, etc., (your losses), then I need to love the ones that are in my life, every where, all around me. This so takes me, out of me, which is really what it is all about. Jesus came to serve us, not be served and He is our example.

If we extrapolate the message of this song through the eyes of Christianity, it is saying that when we are not in our comfort zone, or doing what we want, can we be comfortable where we are? Can we accept that what we are doing, and not really wanting to do, is possibly a huge part of God's big plan for mine, yours and the whole world's best?? The challenge this week, and forever is: Can you love the one you're with? Can you be content where you are and what you are going through? Can you not try to figure everything out? (Oh gosh, intellectual works!) Can we just trust that God has a perfect plan for each one of us, and although we can't understand some of it, that it is God's best plan for us? And you know, it just might be way better than any plan we would have put together.

Keep Walking...

Philippians 4:11 *Not that I speak in respect of want: for I have learned, in whatsoever state I am, therewith to be content.*

Luke 6:31-35 *And as ye would that men should do to you, do ye also to them likewise. For if ye love them which love you, what thank have ye? for sinners also love those that love them. And if ye do good to them which do good to you, what thank have ye? for sinners also do even the same. And if ye lend to them of whom ye hope to receive, what thank have ye? for sinners also lend to sinners, to receive as much again. But love ye your enemies, and do good, and lend, hoping for nothing again; and your reward shall be great, and ye shall be the children of the Highest: for he is kind unto the unthankful and to the evil.*

Peace and Love.

Keep loving...

(Song - Stephen Stills - Love The One You're With)

WE WILL REJOICE

This is a very special day for me. Twenty seven years ago, Dustin Lewis Bowman was given to me by God. Three years ago, I had to give him back. He now has his perfect home where "God shall wipe away all tears from their eyes; and there shall be no more death, neither sorrow, nor crying, neither shall there be any more pain: for the former things are passed away." (Revelation 21:4) And just to keep focused, "For this is the day the Lord hath made and we will rejoice in it." (Psalm 118:24) You know I never realized until I was typing out this scripture that it says "we" will rejoice (not I). If I have no rejoicing in me, I can join Him (and you) as the "we."

1 Corinthians 15:10 *But by the grace of God I am what I am: and his grace which was bestowed upon me was not in vain; but I laboured more abundantly than they all: yet not I, but the grace of God which was with me.*

This says that we need to accept our reality of "I am what I am." I am a mother who has lost both of her sons. Maybe you have/had major trauma or sickness and life seems to not be working out. Know that God's grace (His divine influence on your heart) is with you, allowing you to continue to move forward in the midst of the battle and allowing you to used by Him as His vessel.

Isaiah 6:8 *Also I heard the voice of the Lord, saying, Whom shall I send, and who will go for us? Then said I, Here am I; send me.*

No matter what our past involves, God takes that live coal and purges our sins. So forget the past and move forward and allow yourself to be "picked" for His good use. There are people that need your testimony! This week we will be studying this scripture:

Keep Walking...

2 Corinthians 1:8-10 *For we would not, brethren, have you ignorant of our trouble which came to us in Asia, that we were pressed out of measure, above strength, insomuch that we despaired even of life: But we had the sentence of death in ourselves that we should not trust in ourselves, but in God which raiseth the dead: Who delivered us from so great a death and doth deliver in whom we trust that he will yet deliver us.*

Thank you for participating with me in walking through this thing called life. I love having your arms on both sides of me while our Shepherd leads us. Let us be good sheep and follow!!

Hebrews 3:14 *...steadfast unto the end!*

WE will rejoice...

THE BEST BREAD

I am rereading a book by Tommy Tenney called "Prayers of a God Chaser." My prayer life needed a spiritual jolt and that holy hunger begin to gnaw at me. Hunger is a weird condition. When hunger is satisfied, it always seems to come back, sometimes with even a greater strength. In teaching about eating disorders, I would always say, "The more you eat, the more you want and the less you eat, the less you want." That pretty much covers it from anorexia to compulsive overeating.

Hunger for God's presence is the one true addiction of the human soul and the only vital life source He created us to crave. The more we "consume" His Word, the more we will want. It brings to mind this scripture:

Psalm 34:8 *O taste and see that the Lord is good: blessed is the man that trusteth in Him.*

As Tommy Tenney says, "This verse marks the divine gateway to holy addiction and Godward obsession. The more you stoke the flames of passion for Him, the more passionately hungry you get." On the other hand, unsatisfied hunger rages at first, but then grows fatally weak, and a numbing begins to set in. Look at any picture of starving people and you will see it in their eyes. It is a lack of life, a lack of hope—dull and lost. "The less you eat, the less you want."

The body begins to adapt to "starvation." As metabolism decreases, the body survives on fewer and fewer nutrients and begins to feed on the body itself to try to keep itself alive. Oh, if we could see how this works in our spiritual life. Have we developed a spiritual anorexia, a listlessness for God and His Word, a numbness to the Holy Spirit, and certainly a lack of life and hope? Or have we replaced God's Word with "empty calories" or junk food that seems to fill us up (and out) but leaves

Keep Walking...

us with a lack of vitality to serve others and represent Him? Do we praise Him when we say a little prayer and it all works out perfectly? That's nice, but what do we do when we are seeking Him and nothing is seemingly changing? Do we give up or do we press in to that throne room of God, never giving up and always expecting His greatest to come?

I love this prayer that former First Lady Eleanor Roosevelt carried that seems to prescribe a divine cure or prevention for spiritual listlessness. It will take godly courage to pray it in faith: "Our Father, who has set a restlessness in our hearts and made us all seekers after that which we can never fully find—keep us at tasks too hard for us, that we may be driven to Thee for strength."

This is definitely medicine that will never allow us to depend on ourselves, but instead, always depend upon Him. Selah.

The best Bread...

Share

I was listening to a radio show on Sunday and the minister talked about how since in Isaiah 55 that God's ways are so much higher than ours that we need to be careful when we "try" to interpret the Bible. He was giving a whole different interpretation of the John the Baptist in prison story, and it really seemed very right on. However, it was very different from what I had been taught. When he mentioned the Isaiah 55 scripture, it dawned on me that even though we can try to figure out exactly what God's Word means, I am not sure our finite minds really even do "Him" justice.

Isaiah 55:8-9 *For my thoughts are not your thoughts, neither are your ways my ways, saith the LORD. For as the heavens are higher than the earth, so are my ways higher than your ways, and my thoughts than your thoughts.*

The whole point I think I got out of it is... well... water. You know, water is perfect when you are thirsty; and water works so well when your plants are wilted; and water is the perfect thing needed for the never ending piles of laundry; and of course, there is hot tea. So water is found most everywhere and works for most every need in the physical realm. I kind of think the Word is like that. It is always "water" and that's the Truth, and it works in every spiritual need which is ultimately every physical need.

With that said, our discussion last week centered on speaking out those fears and things that have us bound and gagged, that we don't want to admit and share because of shame, guilt and pride. When we finally open our mouths and share what is going on, the impact of the situation is greatly diminished.

Keep Walking...

The enemy had us captive with something that really seemed so big; but became so "nothing" when we were able to speak it out. Its false superpower got busted! I am not saying that there are not things that are extremely tough but only that the enemy tends to beef up the impact of oppression that could just snuff us out of any life. When we can share our struggles and then apply the Word, hope and peace is on its way, even in the most dire situations. David addresses this in these scriptures:

Psalm 32:3-5 *When I kept silence, my bones waxed old through my roaring all the day long. For day and night thy hand was heavy upon me: my moisture is turned into the drought of summer. Selah. I acknowledge my sin unto thee, and mine iniquity have I not hid. I said, I will confess my transgressions unto the LORD; and thou forgavest the iniquity of my sin. Selah.*

When we do not confess sin, (fear, pride, guilt, shame etc.) appears to wreak havoc with our health. The enemy wants us to keep quiet so those "mushrooms" can grow overnight and create "fungus among us." When David "roared" instead of confessing, the repercussions were physical and emotional.

Find a supportive "family" whereby you can begin to "expose" those places that have held you captive. It is important to be vulnerable and share with spiritually mature people, that these issues that we think are so big, can be exposed to the power and Spirit of God. There is a saying I love and it goes like this: "A sorrow not shared is doubled and a joy not shared is halved." God's power always makes the "big" things of Satan diminish when we share with our close, mature Christian friends.

I truly love each and every one of you and thank you for sharing your lives, your revelations and your testimonies, big and small, with us all.

Keep sharing...

Keep Walking..

For the Furtherance of the Gospel?

I hope everyone is having a joyous spring day...rain or shine. For us, it has been weeks of rain, but today it is beautiful. You can't have one without the other, otherwise you wouldn't appreciate either. That is how it is with life as well. We wouldn't appreciate the mountaintops if we didn't have valleys. God is about contrast and seasons, blessings and sufferings; and the greatest thing is that He is in the center of it all!

Philippians 1:12-14 *But I would ye should understand, brethren, that the things which happened unto me have fallen out rather unto the furtherance of the gospel; So that my bonds in Christ are manifest in all the palace, and in all other places; And many of the brethren in the Lord, waxing confident by my bonds, are much more bold to speak the word without fear.*

What if you really took this scripture to heart? Believing that everything that has happened to you was for the express purpose of the furtherance of the gospel? It gives a whole new twist on things—if your heart's desire is to serve God!

We see Paul saying that everything he went through was for the manifesting of Christ in the palace and in ALL other places. Wow! He was never concerned about all the trials and suffering he had been through, because he knew beyond a doubt that Jesus was in the center of it all, that he worked for Him, not the other way around!!

Would you rather be rewarded by a paycheck from Walmart or from the Son of God who owns the cattle on a thousand hills, as well as the hills, as well as the grass they are eating, as well as the sun that makes it grow, as well as the rain that brings refreshment and growth... and on and on and on?

Keep Walking...

So you find yourself in situations asking, "Why me God?" His answer is probably, "For the furtherance of the Gospel." Will you take your situation and just let Him use it? Whatever you are going through is valuable to God. He is right there in the center of it all. Things are starting to look up!

Take a few minutes and sing this as a prayer for yourself and all others. I have been singing this for you!

Focus on the Center...

(Song - Jesus At The Center (Decade Version) - Israel Houghton & New Breed)

Overcoming Opposition

Once again, I am stuck on a simple sentence that overtakes me in the simplicity of the gospel. The sentence I read in my devotional, by E. Stanley Jones, was this: "Jesus was crucified on misquotations." This is a message for those of you who feel like you have to live out your life in the face of opposition. Do we meet our opponents, whether they be rebellious children, ungodly spouses, irritating bosses, etc., with their own weapons? Do we fight fire with fire? The answer, if you really look at those words, would be, "Of course not, you will get burned."

Our Christian attitudes, obtained from observing the ways of Jesus, are really our greatest assets. When Pilate sentenced Jesus to death based on misquotations of what Jesus had said, you must look deeper as to see who really won this battle. Jesus conquered Pilate by not being like him. He broke Pilate by letting Pilate break His body, while He kept an unbroken spirit. The unbroken spirit of Jesus overcame Pilate and his empire. Often when we come upon opposition, we let it break our hearts until we become ineffective in our own lives and those with whom we are in relationship.

Jones says, "We must ask, not who crucified Christ but what?" He identifies seven sins that were combined to crucify Jesus:

1) Self-interested, moral cowardice - Pilate

2) Vested class interests - the priests

3) Envy - the priests

4) Faithless friendships - Judas

5) Ignorance - the multitude

6) Indifference - the multitude

7) Race-prejudiced militarism - the Roman soldiers.

Keep Walking...

The probability is that we will have to live out our "abundant life" in the face of evil embodied in one or more of these forms. When we do, then this abundant life meets its cross—its death. If you escape the cross, you escape the resurrection. For without death, there is no resurrection.

So practically, what do we do in the face of ignorant opposition? Simple-- we do as Jesus did - "Father forgive them for they know not what they do." And then He died for them. We can do the same, and some day the resurrection will come. It may take days, weeks or years, but we can wait for *"whatsoever is born of God overcometh the world;"* whatever is born of ignorance perishes. Be patient.

Psalm 30:5 *For his anger endureth but a moment; in his favour is life: weeping may endure for a night, but joy cometh in the morning.*

Morning doesn't have to be a certain time, it is when you wake up. Wake up to the fact that in Him, everything we need as already been accomplished. We may need to sit back and watch the greatest masterpiece, by the Greatest Master, unfold. Don't let misquotations or opposition break your spirit. It might just change a nation!

Be an overcomer...

Always Wash Feet

I was recently studying Galatians 4, Romans 8:1-18, Hebrews 8:10-13, Hebrews 10:16-18 and ended with 2 Corinthians. I think the focus was really about how the law and the new covenant cannot mix!!

The Mosaic covenant contained some 600 plus laws and addressed the needy condition of a declining human race. Jesus was the only one to ever fulfill this covenant. It was spoken by God, written on stone and enforced by blessings on obedience, or curses on disobedience (Deuteronomy 28). The Mosaic law was from a perfect God and was thus perfect. However, man is imperfect (just in case you hadn't figured that out) and thus the purpose was to show that man needed a Savior—the basic Gospel message.

The new covenant was "found" in the old covenant and was always there waiting to be unwrapped and received by faith. Our checklist should now only have one item, "Am I obedient to the faith?" All that is required is obedience in believing that He will be my God, and I will be his child.

Hebrews 8:10 *For this is the covenant that I will make with the house of Israel after those days, saith the Lord; I will put my laws into their mind, and write them in their hearts: and I will be to them a God, and they shall be to me a people:*

Romans 1:5 *By whom we have received grace and apostleship, for obedience to the faith among all nations, for his name:*

Romans 16:26 *But now is made manifest, and by the scriptures of the prophets, according to the commandment of the everlasting God, made known to all nations for the obedience of faith:*

Keep Walking...

Acts 6:7 *And the word of God increased; and the number of the disciples multiplied in Jerusalem greatly; and a great company of the priests were obedient to the faith.*

We can also talk about the "perfect law of liberty" and the "royal law" which seem like an oxymoron. We are not accustomed to the law bearing such positive connotations. As we have studied Galatians, perhaps we can get a better glimpse of why Paul fought with such passionate violence for us Gentiles to not have to abide by the Old Testament laws. The New Testament law is all about love and love alone, and links our personal freedom and liberation to God's Word. That is the heart of the phrase "perfect law of liberty."

James 1:25 *But whoso looketh into the perfect law of liberty, and continueth therein, he being not a forgetful hearer, but a doer of the work, this man shall be blessed in his deed.*

James 2:8 *If ye fulfil the royal law according to the scripture, Thou shalt love thy neighbour as thyself, ye do well:*

The best expression of the royal law is summed up in the thought, "Do you want to be right (checklist on the law sheet) or do you want to have relationship?" Sometimes we try to act so super-spiritual, pious, or use our devotion to God as an excuse to ignore people. Beth Moore states in her study of the book of James, the "I'm too busy looking up to look out, kind of mentality doesn't hold water with Jesus. He'd just as soon pour that water from a pitcher and wash somebody's feet." That really takes the heat off knowing every scripture and proper doctrine before we can serve God. Our best hope in anything we do is to do it with love because we know that love NEVER fails.

1 Corinthians 13:8 *Charity never faileth: but whether there be prophecies, they shall fail; whether there be*

tongues, they shall cease; whether there be knowledge, it shall vanish away.

Romans 13:8 *Owe no man anything, but to love one another: for he that loveth another hath fulfilled the law.*

I pray that the big-legal document of laws that you have in your mind about whether you are doing good or bad gets tossed out this year and gets replaced with one simple word—LOVE. Love God, love others and love yourself. I think sometimes we feel like it is easier to follow 600 laws than to love in every situation, but that is why Jesus left and sent us the Holy Spirit to help us out. Thank you God!!

Love Never Fails...

Keep Walking...

Abused and Forgotten?

It is a beautiful time of year in God's creation. The leaves, the weather, the bright, blue sky are all a reminder that God is faithful and that seasons do change. In spite of the beauty of nature, we may be experiencing a famine in our life just as Joseph did when he was sold into slavery by his own family. I am sure many of us can relate to this in some way. God addresses this in Psalm 105 and I encourage you to read it. My Bible entitles this psalm as "The Eternal Faithfulness of God." With that in mind, I want to encourage you with a few of the verses:

Psalm 105:16-24 *Moreover he called for a famine upon the land: he brake the whole staff of bread. He sent a man before them, even Joseph, who was sold for a servant, Whose feet they hurt with fetters: he was laid in iron: Until the time that his word came: the word of the LORD tried him. The king sent and loosed him; even the ruler of the people, and let him go free. He made him lord of his house, and ruler of all his substance. To bind his princes at his pleasure; and teach his senators wisdom. Israel also came into Egypt; and Jacob sojourned in the land of Ham. And he increased his people greatly; and made them stronger than their enemies.*

Often we hear that God doesn't test us. However, many times in the Bible God did test His people to see where their character and faithfulness laid. This is a very special passage to me in that first God called a famine upon the whole land. He wanted to induce a hunger that only He could satisfy, but initiated it in the natural. He then "chose" Joseph (as He wants to use all of us) to go through an extremely long and tough test. God had a perfect plan going on unbeknownst to all. In the end, nations benefited.

Let's stop right there and ask if you feel like the test has been way too long, way too hard, and confusing to understand? Perhaps you even have a slight distaste for what you are going through, wondering if it could really be God's plan for your life? Well, this story is for you and me; to encourage us to, "...not be weary in well doing: for in due season we shall reap, if we faint not" (Galatians 6:9).

So here we have Joseph, hated, accused and stuffed into a well, sold to merchants as a slave, put in jail by a lying woman, and basically forgotten—for a long time. We can then take great comfort in Psalms 105. We see in verse 19 that the Lord "tried" him. This word "tried" in the Hebrew means to refine, purge, goldsmith. In other words, this is a great thing that will bring us beauty and value if we "allow" it.

Testing caused character development in Joseph and that was God's purpose. Joseph was then able to be used to fulfill the rest of the story. Now for the "shiny, valuable part" found in verses 20-24 that show us when Joseph (or whatever YOUR name is) withstood the test, that afterwards came the loosing, the freedom, the increase and finally was made stronger than his enemies. Take a moment and read the whole chapter and watch for the "eternal faithfulness of the Lord." Don't ever think that what you are going through with God holds no purpose. It is of great value. May we allow God to use us in His full will to accomplish all that He desires, even if it is a little "warm" sometimes. He is faithful.

Abused and not forgotten by God...

Keep Walking...

THREE WORDS

I was talking recently with someone about books and teachings and we decided that it was usually one sentence or one main thought that effected us, never the "whole" book. Of course we know that the only "whole" book in which every word can make a difference is the Bible, but it too has a few powerful things to say in just a few words. One of my favorites is found in Corinthians. I can never seem to get past the first three words:

1 Corinthians 13:8 *Charity (agape love) never faileth...* There are so many situations we find ourselves in that we don't seem to have answers to. But God gives an answer in three words for every situation. Are your children out in left field, does your husband ignore you or seemed to have lost interest, is your boss or co-worker annoying, is your physical or emotional pain unrelenting? "The" answer is unconditional love for others, yourself and God—it never fails.

If your physical pain is unbearable, cry out and tell God how much you love Him and trust Him and you will find relief—His love never fails. Agape love is not based on other's actions or words, it is based on loving them in spite of their actions or word. Is your son or daughter on drugs and you've tried everything? Love them right there with needles in their arms or whatever. God says Love NEVER Fails, so we can't go wrong. Let me in my usual "Mary Pat Greekineese" spell it out: A love feast (love) NEVER causes something to drop away or be driven off of one's course, it never loses or becomes inefficient (faileth).

So, if your spouse says, "You look really ugly today, your hair is a mess and I don't even like you," that you can reply in love with a statement saying, "I so appreciate the time you're taking to talk to me." Evil really can't

Keep Walking..

handle love at all and doesn't know how to respond to it, so love wins (never fails)! Okay, enough weird examples!

When we look at the last verse in chapter 13, we see that faith (can't see it yet), and hope (cheerful endurance) are good, but surrounding someone with a love feast beats it all.

1 Corinthians 13:13 *And now abideth faith, hope, charity, these three; but the greatest of these is charity.*

Three simple but profound words - Love NEVER fails! It works for Jesus when He looks at us, so we might as well pay it forward!!

Keep loving...

HE ALREADY HAS

I want to share pretty much the whole chapter of Jeremiah 33, so you may want to read it to get the full message. I will try to put here what I got out of it in hopes that it will bring refreshment to your valleys!

Jeremiah 33:6 *Behold, I will bring it health and cure, and I will cure them, and will reveal unto them the abundance of peace and truth.*

Jeremiah 33:8 *And I will cleanse them from all their iniquity, whereby they have sinned against me; and I will pardon all their iniquities, whereby they have sinned, and whereby they have transgressed against me.*

If you read Jeremiah 31-33, you will find that God was upset with the Jews because of all their sins and was pretty much going to let the Chaldeans have at them. But God always has a better plan than total destruction, even when we deserve it.

Jeremiah 33:15-16 *In those days, and at that time, will I cause the Branch of righteousness to grow up unto David; and he shall execute judgment and righteousness in the land. In those days shall Judah be saved, and Jerusalem shall dwell safely: and this is the name wherewith she shall be called, The LORD our righteousness.*

In verse 6 above, He says, *"I will cure them, and will reveal unto them the abundance of peace and truth,"* and He is going to do that by sending the Branch of David, called "The LORD, our Righteousness." This is one of the names of Jesus. If you are sick or broken you can't out-do what Jesus has done, or will do, for you. You never have to worry about being healed because He says He will and He cannot lie. Satan lies and, of course, anytime he is moving his mouth in our ears we need to remember that it's a lie. Sometimes I think how stupid

Keep Walking..

we are in listening. I mean whoever listens to people that always lie? Yet we find ourselves leaning in and accepting what he has to say when the Bible flat out says that he is a liar. I digress!

We always seem to be looking for physical healing and praying fervently for it, like if we pray hard enough, God will move. Jesus had already healed us when He said "it is finished."

I guess I just need to say exactly what I need to say and that is, as Christians we can sin out the wazoo, have sickness and in spite of all that, Jesus says He has healed us. He may delay the healing, and certainly repenting will help remove any blocks, but He states that healing is a finished work. I don't have to worry about it; I just need to focus on my relationship with Jesus my Righteousness, Jesus my Healer, Jesus my Peace, Jesus my Victorious Warrior, and Jesus my Provider. Everything I need is in His name.

He was letting the Jews know of the upcoming covenant He was making through Jesus. That covenant is a done deal for us. My part of the covenant, and my only part, is to believe and receive Him. The rest is up to Him. I think I will keep it simple and just work on knowing Him and leave the timing of everything else in His hands

It's a done deal...

Blessed, Broken and Given Away

I am currently reading the book of Mark and I love how it is described by commentators. The book of Mark is the shortest of the Gospels and is considered the Gospel of action, moving rapidly from one scene to another. It is also the Gospel of vividness, with the looks and gestures of Jesus receiving unusual attention. Mark was writing for a Gentile audience so I guess that is why it had to be fast-paced versus the slow, drawn-out style of the Pharisees!! Maybe that is why I like the book of Mark; quick, to the point and moving on to the next.

I was reading chapter 6 which is a story about feeding the five thousand. I will try to highlight how it spoke to me this hot, fine day:

Mark 6:36 *"They have nothing to eat"* (disciples speaking)

Mark 6:37 *"You give them something to eat."* (Jesus speaking)

Mark 6:38 *"How many loaves do you have?"* (again, Jesus speaking)

Mark 6:41 *Jesus blessed and broke the loaves and gave them out* (Jesus)

Mark 6:42 *So they ate and were filled.* (everybody!)

So often we look at situations and people who say they are never going to survive unless something changes; they really need to do something. In this passage, Jesus is telling us to give them something, anything, that we have, no matter how minimal the amount it seems. It might be bread, it might be money, it might be a tired smile—but "you" give them something. If we could take whatever little it is that we have, and do as Jesus did, people would be nourished by His abundance that has

Keep Walking..

been given to us to share. We take what we have and pray as Jesus did. He blessed it, broke it and gave it away.

We are a blessed people if we are in relationship with Jesus. We may be "broken" in so many ways, but then again so was Jesus and He gave it all.

I studied a little more about the word loaves. It is a Greek word that means a raised loaf, but it comes from another Greek word (#142), to lift, to take away, to expiate sin. Oh gosh! I got out my 1936 Webster's dictionary to look up "expiate." It means to "extinguish the guilt of by sufferance of a penalty; to make complete satisfaction; to ward off evil; to purify." Loaves, the Bread of Life, is very significant in this passage. It is not ordinary!

Jesus was asking the disciples how many loaves they had; how much "Word" did they possess? Maybe He was asking them, "How much do you believe in me and what my purpose is for mankind? How much forgiveness do you have for others that comes from Me?" Jesus was blessed and broken and given away to the whole world; for us.

We do have "loaves" to give away if we know Him. God is the One who takes what we are willing to give and multiplies it. Blessed, broken and given away. It's a great "slogan" to live by!

Keep leaving!

Go Viral

There is a scripture that sets the tone for my heart, our conference calls, and the Bible study and that is that we should "look" different than people in the world.

1 Thessalonians 1:6-8 *And ye became followers of us, and of the Lord, having received the word in much affliction, with joy of the Holy Ghost: So that ye were ensamples to all that believe in Macedonia and Achaia. For from you sounded out the word of the Lord not only in Macedonia and Achaia, but also in every place your faith to God-ward is spread abroad; so that we need not to speak anything.*

When hard times come, our countenance should look like it belongs to someone who just birthed their long-awaited child. It is a radiance and a glow that just exudes joy, peace and a trust, that this is the perfect child, and always will be!

Let this scripture plant a seed into your heart (whoops, there goes the seed thing again).

In simple words, it is saying that they had become "Lord followers" in much affliction, albeit with much joy, that they were examples to others in _____ (fill in the name of your city) and then everywhere they went. No one really had to speak a thing, or carry a big Bible, or wear a Jesus pin, or have a fish logo on the back of their car, etc., because their faith in God was like a rampant virus and everyone knew they "had it."

That is my prayer for all of us. That when anyone looks at us, they don't smell a stench of smoke, we don't have the "why me" conversation with everyone, but instead, we reflect a little bit of God's glory; enough that people notice and ask. That is the true, greatest form of evangelism!

Keep Walking..

Go viral...

HURRY UP WITH THE SQUEEZING

I think this is my confession message and I am praying that not only something in it benefits you, but that I might get evermore revelation and transformation in my own life!!

Proverbs 15:33 *The fear of the LORD is the instruction of wisdom; and before honour is humility.*

Okay, I humbly submit to you (Okay Lord—please hurry up with the honor!) my defect that seems to be raging lately. You can pick your own defect, but mine is an unseemly, insatiable, irritability, impatience and snappy-ness towards my husband. I seem to get so annoyed over the least of things. He has difficulty hearing my soft, southern voice so I have to repeat myself 20 times. It is "huh- I didn't hear you" and then me getting louder and louder until I feel like I am yelling.

In other conversations, we talk back and forth and you would think we were talking Chinese. Neither of us can seem to figure out with the other is talking about—despite us "saying it so clearly!" And then here it comes, I feel that feeling like when you are chugging up the largest roller coaster with the big circles and swoops right around the corner—you know it's coming, and for me it's the evil-eyed monster of impatience.

Now, trying to seek God in every area of my life, I had been previously warned to never pray for patience. I knew that if I did, all impatience stored up in hell since creation would be beating my door down. I also knew that if I didn't pray for patience towards the one I love most on earth, that slime and mold and scum would begin to take over my relationship. It is the same with God when we are "patiently" waiting on Him to do something in our lives.

Keep Walking...

We have to pray and trust Him for the timing, and if we don't seek Him, then the slime and mold can begin to destroy THE relationship that is vital to our very life.

Let's discuss the waiting part. Yes, I did humble myself and pray for patience. Let me remind you that patience in the Greek language, in most all of the new Testament it means "cheerful endurance." Really God—cheerful??? I was praying today on my "dog walk" and letting God know that I had not seen any progress in this area. I mean, "Really God, it's getting a little worse - so what's the deal?" I want you to know right now that God is very cool and His ways are higher (and better) than mine! He reminded me about something I had read awhile back, and that is that grapes become wine only when they have been squeezed. I came home and told Rick that I was being squeezed and crushed but that the wine was coming. Maybe I will just go ahead and get the glasses out so when the fruit of the vine comes forth, we can truly celebrate God's perfect timing and ways for our life.

James 1:3-4 *Knowing this, that the trying of your faith worketh patience. But let patience have her perfect work, that ye may be perfect and entire, wanting nothing.*

James lets me know that the unseen outcome of my struggles is what will produce patience. I have to let it work and marinate so that it comes out just right. Then, when it is "done," God will have done such a perfect work that I will get to sit back and humbly not want anything other than His work in my life. Trust me, I tried to get myself patient and it lasted about 43 seconds. God is the one that transforms me, and I also have to be patient with myself in letting Him have His perfect way and timing in delivering me. In the meantime, while we are being squished and squeezed, He is ever trying to teach us more about Him! Lord help me to be a patient student while I wait for patience!!

Currently squeezed but still walking...

Characteristics of a Great Leader

I thought I would talk about Nehemiah a minute. He is somewhat of a very cool guy who expresses the practical, every day, side of our faith in God. He was the James of the Old Testament, challenging the people to show their faith by their works. Before you say ugh, the word "works" means that if God has saved you by His grace (and remember part of the Greek definition of grace is "His reflection in us"), then we shouldn't see a bunch of saved people just sitting around. They need to see the love and experience the goodness, kindness, generosity and prayers of the saints. That my friends is our work!

Nehemiah, through hearing about the devastation of the wall in Jerusalem, was prompted by God to move into action and rebuild. His qualities of leadership, inspirational and organizational skills, and confidence in God's purpose, as well as a quick decisive response to problems, qualifies Him as a great leader. He was a man of God with a self-sacrificing spirit, a goal we should all desire to obtain.

The committed people under Nehemiah's dynamic direction overcame:

<u>Mockery</u>

Nehemiah 2:19-20 *But when Sanballat the Horonite, and Tobiah the servant, the Ammonite, and Geshem the Arabian, heard it, they laughed us to scorn, and despised us, and said, What is this thing that ye do? will ye rebel against the king? Then answered I them, and said unto them, The God of heaven, he will prosper us; therefore we his servants will arise and build: but ye have no portion, nor right, nor memorial, in Jerusalem.*

Keep Walking...

Laziness

Nehemiah 4:6 *So built we the wall; and all the wall was joined together unto the half thereof: for the people had a mind to work.*

Threats of physical attack

Nehemiah 4:17 *They which builded on the wall, and they that bare burdens, with those that laded, every one with one of his hands wrought in the work, and with the other hand held a weapon.*

This is a great example for our lives. We are all called to be leaders in some area of our lives and we are called to be servants in other areas. So often we use the excuse that people are against us, or we are just too tired or sick to do what God has called us to do. If He is calling, then He is providing us everything we need.

If you continue reading Nehemiah, you will find that there are some lasting principles that stand out. First, compassion was his springboard of obedience to God's will. Second, you see the cooperation with others that is required to carry out God's will. Third, confidence coming from prayer and the Word which reveals God's will and fourth, a courage and tenacity to complete what God had called them to do.

There was a battle, as we see in verse 17, and it is important to note, that they were doing God's will; rebuilding while fighting. Don't ever think you aren't doing God's will because you are in the heat of the battle. It might be that you are walking in the footsteps of Nehemiah and God is well pleased at your rebuilding process!

And my book signing scripture...

Hebrews 3:14 *For we are made partakers of Christ, if we hold the beginning of our confidence stedfast unto the end;*

Keep walking...

Mirror, Mirror

I pray you are receiving the free gift of God's peace in your life this week. I am in Virginia visiting my family and always trying to put relationships first. As I think on relationships, the first and foremost one is with God. My mantra has become, "Trust God, walk in faith and never give up." We are to reflect God on this earth and Jesus came to show us that a flesh and blood man could do it if He trusted in His Father's will for His life.

That brings me to the mirror of faithfulness. The word says that "He is faithful" and we need to mirror that back and have faith in Him. These three scriptures describe His faithfulness towards us:

Deuteronomy 7:9 *Know therefore that the LORD thy God, he is God, the faithful God, which keepeth covenant and mercy with them that love him and keep his commandments to a thousand generations.*

1 Corinthians 10:13 *There hath no temptation taken you but such as is common to man: but God is faithful, who will not suffer you to be tempted above that ye are able; but will with the temptation also make a way to escape, that ye may be able to bear it.*

1 John 1:9 *If we confess our sins, he is faithful and just to forgive us our sins, and to cleanse us from all unrighteousness.*

Now let's look at this a little closer. Yes we have faith in Him, believing for those things not seen (Rom 4:17). Well, if He is faithful towards us, then He is believing for things in us that He cannot yet see. In other words, He is not expecting us to be perfect, healed, patient, etc., every minute, but has faith that each day we are becoming more and more like Him. He is hopeful towards us and trusting us even when He can't see it yet.

Keep Walking...

Mirror God's faithfulness and know that the reflection is always believing for His transforming power. Even though we are not perfectly believing in Him in faith, He is perfectly believing in us. What a deal!

Mercy...

Keep Walking..

How am I Known?

I had a wonderful visit with a very special friend and it prompted me to write about what the most important thing in our Christian walk is. It's to focus on love, relationships, true caring and intimate time with others. It was a very special time because we took the time to visit with one another. It would have been easier for me to just send a card but it was important that I was there for her (and her for me)! We spent all day laughing, crying, sharing and trying to figure out God. It was a priceless time and I will always be grateful for it. The other reason this is on my mind is I had been meditating on the scripture and song that says, "They will know we are Christians by our love."

John 13:34-35 *A new commandment I give unto you, That ye love one another; as I have loved you, that you also love one another. By this shall all men know that ye are my disciples, if ye have love one to another.*

Many of you have listened to my CD/DVD, "Biblical Incites to Food and Related Issues." In it, I talk about how many of us become "known" by what we eat, i.e., the vegetarian, the junk food eater, the organic one, the healthy one, etc. We do the same thing with "other" religions (yes, food was my religion for a long time). I began to think about everything religious people "put on" so we know them. The Jews avoid pork and shellfish, the Baptists proclaim they don't drink, the Episcopalians and Catholics love to drink but wear fancy robes when they preach, the non-denominational sects preach in t-shirts and flip flops to appeal to the young. The list goes on and on.

What the scripture above says is that people will know us by our love and our expression of it to others, not by all this other stuff that religion tries to show. We find that

Keep Walking...

it easier to have a "law" to express our religion versus the true meaning of Christ in us; His love, and relationship with Him and others. So the questions I have for you is this: Can we lay down all the "things" that we put on trying to show that we are Christians? Or are we going to depend on His flow of love to us and through us? It is certainly worth any amount of time you have to meditate on that.

Who do YOU look like?

(Song - They will know we are Christians by our Love)

NEVER GIVES UP, NEVER RUNS OUT

"How are you?" is a question we are asked on a daily basis. Rick always answers, "Blessed and highly favored," while I say, "I'm good, it's all by faith." Sometimes I am really not so good, but saying that reminds me that we have to call those things that are not as if they were. So by faith, I am good and I hope you are as well! Remember faith is the substance of things hoped for, the evidence of things not seen (Hebrews 11:1)

Some days, I feel a little apathetic, or really just not caring, or just going through the motions knowing that this too shall pass if I just "keep walking," even if I would rather not. My thoughts often begin to think about the loss of my sons, and then trying to figure out what could have happened and why. Boy, is that ever a way to open the door to begin to doubt God's plan for your life in the midst of your circumstances.

Yesterday my pastor talked on the book of Ruth, chapter one, and it was the "divine appointment" of encouragement that I needed. If you don't know the story of Ruth, I encourage you to read the whole book as to understand this message. Here are a few verses so you will get the gist:

Ruth 1:8 *The LORD deal kindly with you* (She knows the goodness of God)

Ruth 1:13 *For it grieves me very much for your sakes that the hand of the LORD has gone out against me!*

Ruth 1:20 -21 *Do not call me Naomi (pleasant, delightful, lovely) ; call me Mara (bitterness) for the Almighty has dealt very bitterly with me. I went out full, and the LORD has brought me home again empty. "Why do you call me Naomi, since the LORD has testified against me, and the Almighty has afflicted me?"*

Keep Walking...

Naomi knows His goodness, but she has just experienced famine, death, and loss of her husband and two sons. She reflects human nature in general as she blames God. Her words come in her bewilderment of her situation and she hopelessly looks at the future as a widow. Ruth, a widowed Moabite, and pagan daughter-in-law, was drawn by something greater than Naomi's misery as she tells Naomi that she will follow her. She was drawn by God saying, "Your God will be my God."

Naomi felt "finished" and her behavior was probably pretty "mopey." However, God still had a mighty purpose in her life. We know that even in the pits of situations, God orders all the circumstances of daily life, even for the most seemingly unimportant people. So Ruth, drawn by the God that Naomi served, was woven into the great tapestry of God's plan of salvation for us all. Descended from Ruth (a pagan you remember) was King David, and from the line of David comes the Messiah himself.

God dramatically reveals His will that human loss is always recoverable and that we can work with Him in extending such possibilities to those in need. If you are feeling "over" with God, please know that He has given us this story to show a fruitful end to a devastating story. If that was too deep of a revelation, maybe you can get it this way: God took a "whiny and my life stinks and is over" person and caused a pagan women to see Him in her and brought a Savior forth from her lineage.

You never know what people see even if we can't see it ourselves.

"His love never fails, never gives up and never runs out on me." You know how I love music. May this song minister to the depths of your hurts and losses and give you an excitement that even though we may never see it, we are a huge part of God's plan.

Tight hugs.

(Song - One Thing Remains – Kristian Stanfill)

Just Come

Matthew 11:28-29 *Come unto Me, all ye that labour and are heavy laden, and I will give you rest. Take my yoke upon you, and learn of me; for I am meek and lowly in heart: and ye shall find rest unto your souls.*

"Come to me," "Learn of me," and "I will give you rest." Come—learn—rest; wow, that seems too simple! What about all the questions I have? What about all the work You want me to do? What about my need to figure out Your plan for my life? "The questions that truly matter in life are remarkably few, and they are all answered by these words, "Come to Me." (Oswald Chambers, My Utmost for His Highest, June 11)

I started reading in the book of Joshua this morning and the same theme kept arising. God had appeared to Joshua as the "captain of the host of the Lord" (Josh. 5:14). It was Joshua's task, as it is ours, not so much to follow the Captain's plans, as to know the Captain. We need to be on His side, not He on ours. We need peace; He is peace. We need strength; He is our strength. We need healing; He is our healing, and on and on. HE is what we need, not something He has. As I often say, "We need to appropriate and become one with all that Jesus has already done.

I would like to ask you this question: "Do we have more faith in our works for Jesus than faith in what He did for us?" Again, simply, "Come to Me." My new favorite memory verse is this:

Psalm 61:2 *When my heart is overwhelmed; lead me to the rock that is higher than I.*

We don't necessarily need to pray more, or read more, or volunteer for vacation Bible school. We need to go straight to The Rock. The question for the week is this:

Keep Walking...

Can we lay down all our works and spiritual drivenness and simply come to Him? If we can do this, He promises us that He will give us rest. Maybe religious spirits have had their time in our lives long enough!

Just come...

The Crucible of Life

Job was not meant to know the explanation of his sufferings. There are some things about human suffering God cannot possibly explain to us at the time without destroying the very purpose it was designed to fulfill. Can we be OK with that? God is involved in human affairs. Job and his grief meant enough to God to cause Him to speak. God's purpose was to bring Job to the end of his own self-righteousness, self-vindication and self-wisdom, so he could find his all in God. That feels harsh when we already feel like we are good Christians, trying to do the right thing. But God wanted 100% of Job, every part of his being. Maybe that is a huge compliment!

When deep suffering threatens the foundation of our faith, as was the case with Job, it can destroy us unless we are firmly rooted in God's Truth. In times of tragedy, we face the temptation of making God our adversary instead of our advocate. We can focus on declaring our innocence and questioning the justice of God, or we can bow in humility and wait for God to reveal Himself and His purpose to us. The struggle of faith is a personal one. We each enter the crucible of life alone. We must test the mettle of our faith in God against uncontrollable forces, and win our individual victories. There will be times when family and friends may be taken from us and we must stand alone... but for God! We must never forget that God is in control of every situation.

No matter what you are going through, if you will just trust in Him, all things will work together for His greatest purpose in our lives. Sometimes that is a hard thing to swallow when you are going through devastating times. But then God gives us "Living Water" to drink. We will and can flourish in all things if we believe His greatest will is being accomplished.

Keep Walking...

Job 12:10 *In whose hand is the soul of every living thing, and the breath of all mankind.*

Keep walking...

A Great Ending

Are you excited about where you are in life? You may say, "Well not really. I long for the good old days, when my husband was still here or I hadn't lost my house to foreclosure or my kids to drugs," or whatever in your life seems to be stealing your joy. The Bible says that the thief comes to steal, kill and destroy (John 10:10) and with all due respect the devil does do his job with excellence. The question becomes, "Are we as believers, doing our job in believing the rest of that scripture; believing in He who gives life and life more abundantly, even when times in our life are so dark?" We can believe in abundant life or abundant destruction and that is OUR choice.

In thinking about the word "stealing" there is always the chance that you may get it back. The police may find your stolen car, your stolen health may be returned, your kids may come home, etc. If you trust God more than the enemy it is a guaranteed return! If the thief is whispering in your ear that the best days are over, I want you to do me (and you) a favor and say these verses out loud:

Job 42:12 *So the LORD blessed the latter end of Job more than his beginning...*

Ecclesiastes 7:8 *Better is the end of a thing than the beginning thereof and the patient in spirit is better than the proud in spirit.*

No matter where you are in the battlefield of life, etch these scriptures in your heart. No matter how good your life used to be, or is now; the end is going to supersede your greatest expectation. Encourage yourself in this Word and be patient. God is working out something spectacular that our wildest and greatest desires cannot fathom.

Keep Walking...

One day I was riding my bike and praying out of a deep and sorrowful place when God spoke. He whispered in my ear, "I am the Alpha and Omega, the Beginning and the End, and you are in the middle. Keep walking."

Book ended by God!

Keep Walking..

BOOKS AND RESOURCES

Walking Through Fiery Trials

Walking Through Fiery Trials is Mary Pat's story of this challenging journey through death and its torment - faith and its triumph. She shares her heart with gut-wrenching transparency.

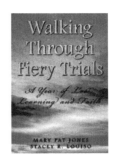

No Shuffling... no pink fuzzy slippers

This teaching originated from the writing of her book which offers encouragement and ministry to those going through their own fiery trials. It is an in-depth study and reflection of what God's Word says about sorrow and loss. God gave Mary Pat this message and it catapulted her out of the devastation and despair of losing her mother and both sons all within one year. This teaching can be used in a Bible study format or small groups.

Biblical Insights to Food and Related Issues

An insightful and surprising teaching that God gave Mary Pat after deliverance from her past history with eating disorders and addictions. She has a Master's of Science degree in Nutrition and is a Registered Dietitian; she also has worked in natural and alternative medicine for decades. After all her training in those

Keep Walking...

fields, and comparing those methods to what the Bible declares, she believes most food issues are spiritually rooted and that current nutritional teaching contains a considerable amount of deception. This teaching is available on CD and offers ministry time at the end.

What Do You Do When Your world Falls Apart?
ebook available on www.creativefootage.org.

For more details or to purchase any of these products or services visit our website at:

www.creativefootage.org

CONTACT

Creative Footage
Mary Pat Jones
150 Roland Rd.
Thomaston, GA 30286
(706) 646-4908

email: jones1885@gmail.com
www.creativefootage.org
www.stillmeadowscabins.com

Keep Walking...

Keep Walking..

Made in the USA
Columbia, SC
17 February 2019